CURIOUS
BUCKINGHAMSHIRE

CURIOUS
BUCKINGHAMSHIRE

ROGER LONG

PHOTOGRAPHY BY BRENDA ALLAWAY
COMPILATION BY DAVE BLACKMAN

The
History
Press

First published 2010

The History Press
The Mill, Brimscombe Port
Stroud, Gloucestershire, GL5 2QG
www.thehistorypress.co.uk

Typesetting and origination by The History Press
Printed in Great Britain

CONTENTS

ALSO BY ROGER LONG

A Grim Almanac of Old Berkshire
Curious Oxfordshire
Historic Inns Along the River Thames

AUTHOR'S NOTE

Right, here we go again, another local book; this time I have inflicted myself on unsuspecting Buckinghamshire. I mentioned in my last book that the original intention was to do a book on all that is Curious in Berks, Bucks and Oxon. However, as I collected stories from literally hundreds of outlets it soon became apparent that the volume would extend over some 400-500 pages, hence the three separate books, *A Grim Almanac of Old Berkshire*, *Curious Oxfordshire* and now *Curious Buckinghamshire*.

'What next?' I hear you shout in eager anticipation. The answer is that I am not sure. I have started collating substance for a possible 'Curious Hampshire'; however, I have already been inundated with material from all over the county and we are already looking at 300 pages. Hence there is a strong probability that I shall have to divide the work into 'Curious Towns of Hampshire' and 'Curious Villages of Hampshire'.

I am often asked where the stories come from. The answer is from all over the place, often pubs, but this source is rapidly drying up (no pun intended) as we lose more and more hostelries on a daily basis. Old newspapers are quite informative, but one can sift for days without finding anything interesting if you are unlucky. Word of mouth is another source, but facts, fiction and exaggeration are difficult to separate or evaluate. Obviously some of my tales have been related before in other books; I hope I have named and honoured the principal author in these instances. I flatter myself that a high percentage of the stories in *Curious Buckinghamshire* have never seen the light of day other than in local newspapers. Also, uniquely, I have visited every site mentioned. I enjoy what I do or I wouldn't do it. I hope it also gives the reader some pleasure.

Roger Long

1

SOUTH BUCKINGHAMSHIRE

AMERSHAM

A footpath from the town leads to Amersham Hill, where, in the sixteenth century, William Tylsworth, with others, was burnt at the stake. Tylsworth was a Lollard, one of a group that followed John Wycliffe, the reformer who attacked the dogmas of the Church and the powers of the priests. Tylsworth's executioners added a terrible and sadistic twist to his fate by forcing his young daughter to ignite the faggots on which he perished.

William Tylsworth is thought by some to be the ghostly figure that has been detected at the Chequers Inn at Amersham. The Chequers has been so malignantly haunted by a grieving spectre of a man and the terrified screams of a woman that at least one landlord took to his heels. The awesome malevolence of the spectres at the inn has necessitated several exorcisms and the services of a medium over the years. In 1971 a barman saw quite distinctly the figure of a cloaked man attempting to ascend the chimney.

A more popular candidate than Tylsworth for the Chequers' ghost is a man named Osman or Auden. Osman was Tylsworth's gaoler when the unfortunate man was lodged at the inn the night prior to his execution. Tylsworth was accompanied by five other men and a woman, all destined to join him in his terrible fate. Tradition has it that Osman wrestled with his conscience the whole of the night; he had several opportunities to let his prisoners escape, but decided against it. The phantom of the chimney is thought to personify Osman's attempt to escape his own conscience.

The horrific screams that put landlords to flight are thought to be the same as those that emanated from Tylsworth's daughter when Osman informed her that she was to initiate her father's death.

A more benign and friendly ghost resides at the delightful seventeenth-century Crown Hotel at Amersham. The Crown was once a staging inn and also served as a courtroom for the local magistrates. The shade of an old grey lady is said to frequent the curiously named Quacks Room, and also a couple of other bedrooms at the further end of the hotel. Locals believe that the ancient crone was once

The Chequers at Amersham is said to be haunted by William Tylsworth.

The Crown at Amersham is said to be haunted by a tidy-minded old lady.

a maid at the Crown. This is certainly suggested by the lady's habits; she has been known to tidy clothes left lying around by guests and to pack them into drawers and wardrobes. All very helpful, but the old lady also shows touches of inquisitiveness verging on the nosy; she often inspects and scrutinises articles of clothing and jewellery.

Bendrose House at Amersham has been the home of two very different celebrities: Oliver Cromwell in the seventeenth century and Dirk Bogarde in the twentieth. The old farmhouse has a very unusual manifestation indeed. Apart from the more frequently experienced scrapings, scufflings and footsteps, inhabitants of Bendrose House have experienced electrical-type shocks. The sensation, which can last for up to four minutes, has been encountered by six or seven guests simultaneously in different rooms of the house. The time of these experiences has always been between four and five o'clock in the morning.

For years religion was a controversial subject in Amersham. The persecution of Lollards and Quakers had reached drastic proportions. One day, a magistrate indulging himself at the Griffin Inn in the old part of the town noticed a Quaker funeral approaching. The cortège was obviously making its respectable journey to the Friends meeting house on the Wycombe Road. However, with chicken drumstick and ale mug in hand, the magistrate emerged from the inn and put a stop to the funeral. The coffin lay beside the road for three days.

According to Christopher Winn's excellent book, *I Never Knew That about England*, Ruth Ellis (1927-1955), the last woman hanged in Britain, rests in Amersham's St Mary's churchyard.

The 'Cunning Man' was held in awe throughout Europe in the eighteenth and nineteenth centuries. The wizard was the local philosopher, veterinary surgeon, dentist, legal interrogator and astrologer. He knew the powerful ingredients of herbs and flowers. However, when dealing with the uneducated peasants he often played the showman, introducing somewhat ridiculous rites that might or might not cure the affected. In an extremely elaborate and complicated ceremony at Amersham, the Cunning Man measured a healthy and an ailing boy with a stick. He then danced around with the stick above his head muttering incantations. He then buried the stick, symbolically interring the curse. The outcome of the 'cure' is unknown.

Seventy-four-year-old Herbert Baker was a retired banker. He lived in harmony with his second wife Helen Davidson, a local and well-respected doctor, who had kept her maiden name probably because of her reputation for being very good at her chosen profession. On Wednesday 9 November 1966 at 1.35 p.m. Herbert left for his part-time job. When he returned later that afternoon he was mildly surprised by Helen's absence. Her car was gone, as was their wire-haired terrier, Fancy. Herbert initially assumed she had been called out by a patient and had

Ruth Ellis, the last woman to be hanged in England, rests in Amersham's St Mary's churchyard.

Cunning Men were usually respected but generally lived the life of a recluse. *(Brenda Allaway)*

taken the dog for a walk afterwards. However, as time wore on he became a little more concerned and organised a brief but unsuccessful search with friends. Herbert later telephoned the police.

Helen Davidson's Hillman car was found in a lay-by near Hodgemoor Wood on the Amersham to Beaconsfield Road. The car was locked and had the doctor's personal belongings inside. A search began at 8 a.m. the next morning and Helen Davidson's body was discovered in the nearby woods at 2.15 that afternoon. Fancy, her dog, had remained with her all night. Following the discovery of the body Scotland Yard was contacted, for it was obvious that Helen Davidson had been murdered in a particularly brutal way.

It was thought that Helen had been killed by being struck with a blunt weapon on the front of her head. The skull had been fractured and she would have died instantly. However, this did not stop the killer continuing with the frenzied attack.

Fancy made it difficult for police to remove Helen, until finally through thirst and hunger she left her mistress's side to be fed and watered at the local police station. Soon the murder weapon was discovered; it was a 3ft charred branch from a poplar tree. The choice of weapon would seem to suggest that the attack was spontaneous and not premeditated. At Amersham Hospital a post-mortem performed by Dr David Bowen confirmed the cause of death. He also discovered a bruise or scorch mark on the neck which he deemed to have been caused by the rubbing of the strap of the binoculars Helen Davidson had been wearing. An inch-by-inch search of Hodgemoor Woods was conducted, involving up to forty police officers with dogs.

Through their enquiries, the police were able to work out Helen's movements on the fatal day. At 2.30 p.m. she had visited several patients in Amersham. Later she was witnessed purchasing some milk at the Express Dairy in Hill Avenue. More witnesses put the doctor in Amersham at 3.45 p.m., this time driving up Gore Hill, which leads to Hodgemoor Woods, the scene of the fatality – in all probability to give Fancy some fresh air.

Very little came from the police investigation, despite the local newspapers giving every possible assistance. It seemed to be a motiveless crime. A crime of opportunity was suspected but nothing was stolen from the car or the body. One rather far-fetched theory was that a couple out courting had noticed her with the binoculars, and, suspecting she was a private detective employed by someone's husband or wife, killed her. It was also suggested that the killer could have been an ex-patient who had either been mis-diagnosed or poorly treated by Helen Davidson, and attacked her for revenge. However, nothing in her past could be found to substantiate this theory. Obviously, though, she must have been attacked by a local; no stranger would have been familiar with the scene of the crime. The enquiry virtually ground to a halt and after three months Scotland Yard officers were recalled. This left the case in the hands of the local officers from Amersham, Detective Inspector Lund and Detective Sergeant Dale.

There was some slight activity when the *News of the World* offered a reward for information in 1974. But the re-ignition of the case was momentary and soon died. Later, there was hope of an arrest of a man who had moved to Australia shortly after the event. He was known for extreme violence, a fact which did not take long for the Australian police to become aware of. The gentleman returned to England, where, in 1980, he was accused of striking an old man over the head with an iron bar. He was later pulled over by the police for a motoring offence and enquired of the officers why they were bothering him instead of discovering the murderer of Dr Davidson; a very strange thing to ask some thirteen years after the offence. In November 1980 Mr X was taken in for questioning concerning the murder of Helen Davidson. However, after forty-eight hours he was released without charge and the murderer of the well-respected doctor, Helen Davidson, remains at large.

ASHLEY GREEN

Although Berkhamsted Castle (built by William the Conqueror in the eleventh century for his brother) is just over the Hertfordshire border (and so strictly speaking should not be mentioned in this book), it is reputed that a secret tunnel ran from it to Ashley Green in Buckinghamshire. Many colourful characters stayed at the castle during its illustrious history, including Thomas Becket, Geoffrey Chaucer, the Black Prince, Piers Gaveston and three of Henry VIII's wives. A less happy resident was King John of France who was imprisoned here after the Battle of Poitiers.

Today there is little left of the castle other than earth mounds and a few pieces of scattered masonry. The tunnel is thought to have been intended to follow a ley line to Bix in Oxfordshire. If so, it was a very ambitious project indeed. It is believed that at least part of the passage was made up of the natural tunnels caused by the underground rivers and streams that are common in this part of the country. The story goes that after heavy rain the tunnel was submerged, but was perfectly serviceable most of the time. No one is sure where the entrance of the tunnel is. A consensus of opinion believes it to be on a small piece of land now owned by the Water Board.

I had long known about the supposed tunnel at Ashwell Green. However, the Women's Institute publication, *The Buckinghamshire Village Book*, informed me of another curiosity to be found at Ashwell Green: the pudding stone. A pudding stone is a conglomerate of pebbles in a siliceous matrix (yes I had to look it up).

Ashley Green, village of mysteries.

Ashley Green's uninspiring pudding stone.

It is said that the stone is somehow able to tell the depth of a nearby well. Apparently the stone's original position was where three ley lines met. The village church was built on the spot.

BEACONSFIELD

There is reputed to be a ghost at the Chilton Cinema at Beaconsfield. It is presumed to be Walter Gay, who managed the building in the 1960s. Most of Walter's tricks were harmless, but once he caused some financial inconvenience when he shut the cinema for the afternoon by closing the mechanical curtains part-way through a performance. The curtains refused to budge and the customers had to be refunded.

Gay is quite a well-attested apparition. His slight figure and grey hair have been described by half a dozen different witnesses on as many occasions. One of the manager's most vivid performances was when an usherette noticed him seated near the front of the auditorium. Thinking at first it was a sleeping customer the usherette continued to clear the remainder of the theatre. When she returned some minutes later Walter had absconded. The phantom manager does not appear to restrict his manifestations specifically to the theatre building. A lady that lived in the flat above also had several visitations. They seemed to coincide with the appearance of female visitors.

Beaconsfield, once home to Enid Blyton, Edmund Waller, Edmund Burke, Robert Frost and G.K. Chesterton, has a propensity for charming old inns, which may have been the attraction for at least some of those named above.

A less welcome visitor was Moses Hatto (*see* Burnham), who was briefly lodged in the small Beaconsfield lock-up. Hatto, the murderer of Mary Anne Sturgeon, spent his days in Beaconsfield hurling verbal abuse at those who came within earshot.

At the George Inn, at Beaconsfield, sword cuts on the stairs can be seen. It is claimed that Claude Duval, the famous highwayman, made them whilst fighting off the Bow Street Runners.

Terry Pratchett, the world-famous science-fiction writer, was born in Beaconsfield in 1945.

BLEDLOW

Bledlow sits on a steep spa of the Chilterns. It looks across a vale and is near the vicinity of the Icknield Way. On the side of the hill, and acting as a landmark, is a huge Greek cross – Bledlow's Cross. The carving is about 25ft wide and is almost, but not quite, unique; it has a neighbour, Whiteleaf Cross. These two are the only turf-cut crosses in the country.

Close by the Upper Icknield Way is a Bronze Age barrow known locally as 'The Cop'. There are also signs of very early habitation at Bledlow Ridge. The name Bledlow Ridge means 'bloody hill', a name which is said to commemorate a terrible battle between the Saxons and the Danes. The village is mentioned in the Domesday Book but there is strong belief that there was a settlement high on the Ridge as early as 300 BC.

It is known that there was a mighty battle at nearby Chinnor in 1643, which resulted in a rare Royalist victory. Remnants from the Civil War are still regularly discovered here, varying from coins to cannonballs. I have been informed that a sword was found comparatively recently in an Elizabethan farmhouse where Cromwell stabled his horse. There have been reports of a ghostly army marching along Bledlow Ridge. It is heard more frequently than seen, but personally I have been unable to find any witnesses whatsoever. If there is a phantom army it could be from any time or nationality; Danes, Saxons or Romans could be likely candidates or possibly even Royalists or Roundheads.

BURNHAM

Burnham Abbey Farm was the scene of a horrific murder in November 1854. The farm owner, a man named Goodwin, returned home one night to find his men fighting a fire that emanated from a top bedroom. The fire was easily arrested but in its wake the assembled men found the body of the attractive housekeeper, thirty-six-year-old Mary Anne Sturgeon. The poor woman had been bludgeoned to death and then her body covered in napkins and finally set alight. The heat had been to such an extreme that the bottom half of the body had completely burnt away. A twenty-six-year-old stable hand and manservant named Moses Hatto was arrested for the heinous crime after he had boasted of his involvement at Maidenhead Riverside station. His actions before and after the murder left little doubt that he was guilty and an unrepentant Hatto was hanged at Aylesbury some two weeks later. It is thought to be the ghost of Moses Hatto that walks a pathway between Burnham and Cippenham. It was this route that he took in life whilst exercising Goodwin's dogs. A full account of this atrocious murder is related in my book *I'll Be Hanged*.

'The Pope is a Knave' was carved on one of the pillars of the church. The story goes that the inscriber returned to the church after imbibing at the Old Five Bells opposite. He then inscribed on the same pillar, but with less accuracy, 'The Pope is a villin'.

Maidenhead's Riverside station, where Moses Hatto boasted of committing murder.

Burnham church, where 'The Pope is a knave' is inscribed on one of the pillars.

The Old Five Bells, where the inscriber of 'The Pope is a villin' imbibed.

CHALFONT ST PETER

It is a case of the tune having ended but the melody lingering on at the fourteenth-century White Hart at Chalfont St Peter. An ex-landlord, Donald Ross, is thought to be the purveyor of the spooky violin music that occasionally reverberates around the inn. Ross died not long after the First World War. Up to his death he regularly used to entertain his customers on a violin. The word 'entertain' however is subject to interpretation; opinions differed as to the landlord's accomplishment on his chosen instrument. One report states that Ross spent hours practising his art upstairs while thirsty customers hammered empty glasses on the bar to attract his attention. Donald Ross is also thought to be responsible for the ghostly footsteps that are heard in the first-floor corridor. The footsteps are usually heard at about 4 a.m. There is also a slightly more frightening story, one that suggests the spirits at the White Hart are plural rather than singular. In 1980 a landlord at the inn awoke to see three apparitions beside his bed; they promptly disappeared before his eyes – the time was about 4 a.m.

Not to be outdone by the White Hart, the Greyhound public house just down the road also has associations with the supernatural. A coach and four is said to speed towards any late-night revellers who are walking the highway near the

The White Hart at Chalfont St Peter, where ghostly violin music is heard.

Be careful of the ghostly coach and horses when crossing the road near the Greyhound Inn at Chalfont St Peter.

The obelisk at
Chalfont St Peter.
(*Brenda Allaway*)

Greyhound. One apparently needs a cool head and a stoic nature, because if one stands firm the coach disappears a split second before impact.

The obelisk at Chalfont St Peter was erected by Sir H.T. Gott in 1785. It was said to mark the position where King George III slew a mighty stag. On the face of it this would seem to be a rather grandiose embellishment for such a trivial deed. However, it was adopted as a signpost to various local towns. When it was restored in 1899 it was discovered that it was intended to be a beacon for lighting the streets of the dark town.

There is another story concerning George III. It is said that the king had been hunting in the area when he was separated from his entourage by thick fog. He accosted a local yokel and asked him where he was. The yokel replied, 'Peters is down there and Giles over yonder, but this ere ain't rightly a place at all'. The king replied that he would make it a place and had the obelisk constructed to mark the spot.

CHENIES

Chenies Manor House stands in the delightful village of Chenies. Until recently it was owned by the Dukes of Bedford, having been bought by their predecessor, John Russell, in 1530 so that he could lavishly entertain Henry VIII. Catherine Howard and Anne Boleyn both slept here on occasions, as did Elizabeth I.

A less happy guest at Chenies Manor was Charles I. He was a captive of the Parliamentarians and was at Chenies under house arrest. It is thought to be Charles' unquiet spirit that is responsible for the phantom footsteps that are often heard emanating from a bedroom, the spirit of the unhappy king pacing the floor in desperation.

A more recent story that may just be a variation on a haunting theme concerns some minor refurbishment to Chenies. Recent owners decided to fit a wardrobe in the bedroom. On taking measurements, they found the room to be smaller internally than it was deemed to be by the external compilations. Demolition work revealed an ancient prayer-cell with a date carved into the wall. The story goes that, shortly after the discovery, the host threw a party. In order to accommodate all his guests, the owner was forced to sleep in the now extended prayer-cell.

A strange secret room was discovered at the Tudor manor house at Chenies.

He read for a while by candlelight before locking the door. In the morning he awoke with a shudder, finding both door and window mysteriously open. Incidentally the day and the month were the same as the ones carved into the wall.

This story sounds a little too pat for me. Firstly, in this massive house could the owner really find nowhere else to sleep? Also, did he not realise that the night of the party coincided with the date carved in the ex prayer-cell? Lastly, if a man can see, let alone be able to read, by candlelight after a party he certainly doesn't go to the sort of party that I do.

CHESHAM

Chesham is a charming and cheerful little town that has produced many characters. One of the most colourful was Roger Crab who opened a hat shop here in 1651.

Roger Crab was quite a wealthy man, but being eccentric to the extreme he sold his estates and distributed his money to the poor. Keeping the hat shop in Chesham, he retired to a cottage he built himself near Uxbridge. He then adopted his own form of Christianity, which forbade him to eat flesh or drink alcoholic liquor. He lived on herbs, grassroots, cabbages, bread and bran. Crab became a recluse, donned himself only in sackcloth and wrote a book called *The English Hermite*. His strange ideas made him famous the length and breadth of the country and his forthright and outspoken opinions got him into several altercations with legal authorities. Roger Crab's book is virtually unheard of now, but he will live on forever in another, as he was the model for the Mad Hatter in Lewis Carroll's *Alice in Wonderland*.

In an ancient Berkshire and Buckinghamshire magazine I came across a photograph of a freak animal and a billboard advertisement describing it. The animal, which was apparently born with a litter of healthy pigs, was described thus:

> The most outstanding phenomena from Henry Deans, Chesham, Bucks. Consisting of five different species. Two heads the one resembling an elephant and rat with the eyes which are similar to those of an owl the other that of a pig except for the nose and eyes which resemble that of a dog. Both heads are in opposite directions.

Henry Dean goes on to describe the bodies as perfect, 'growing from the shoulders to tails and eight legs'. Obviously the freak animal was one of many that are born each year and quickly disposed of, but in the 1850s they were a source of financial gain. A note at the foot of the article announces one redeeming feature. It states that since 1856 the freak became the property of a local man who exhibited it for the benefit of charitable causes.

Lewis Carroll is thought to have based his Mad Hatter on Roger Crab at Chesham. (*Brenda Allaway*)

THE MOST
ASTOUNDING PHENOMENON
OF THE DAY!

FROM

Henry Dean's, Chesham, Bucks,

Consisting of FIVE DIFFERENT SPECIES, having

TWO HEADS;

The one resembling the Elephant and Rat, with the exception of the eyes, which are similar to those of an Owl; the other, that of a Pig, except the nose and eyes, which resemble those of a Dog. Both heads are in opposite directions; it has

2 Perfect Bodies,

Growing in one of the shoulders, two tails, eight legs and feet perfect, and being small in size, renders it inoffensive and simple in appearance, fitting for any Lady or Gentleman to look at, and patronised by all Schools, and pronounced by the respectable inhabitants of Chesham and its vicinity to be the most

WONDERFUL and BEAUTIFUL CURIOSITY

In nature ever exhibited, well deserving the attention of the public.

Littered with seven other fine and healthy pigs on February 23rd, 1856.

Witness my hand,

HENRY DEAN,

In the employ of Mr. W. Lowndes, Magistrate, of Chesham, Bucks, before whom the above has been exhibited with great satisfaction as a most singular curiosity.

☞ Please to keep this Bill till called for.

An "astounding phenomenon" born in 1856. It has been in the possession of the family of E. F. Norman since 1856 and years ago was often exhibited in the Chesham area for the benefit of charitable causes.

Chesham's freak animal.

In Chesham thieves hopped in through the back of a restaurant and stole 300 pairs of frog legs. The French chef was affronted and criticised the thieves' lack of taste. I quote, 'What really annoys me is that [they] forgot the sauce ... and you can't serve frog legs without sauce Provencal.'

DOWNLEY

The Women's Institute's *The Buckinghamshire Village Book* states that there was once a man in the village called Jimmy Two-bits. The chap got his strange nickname in a most unusual way. Legend dictates that Jimmy was by the fire one Sunday morning when his wife enquired how the meat was cooking. Jimmy lifted the lid and asked, 'Which bit?' He was then informed by his wife that there was only one bit. Her husband assured her that he could count two. It turned out that a frog had been inadvertently put in with the water from the well.

Live jumping meat at Downley. (*Brenda Allaway*)

FAWLEY

There is an eerie mausoleum in the churchyard at Fawley housing the Freemans who ran Fawley Court for over 200 years. Despite efforts from the Church and local council, the door to the mausoleum is forever being broken in. There have been rumours of witchcraft ceremonies here. If so, it is a near perfect setting – 'ominous' is not too strong a word for the site.

Just as eerie and atmospheric is the Temple at Fawley Court. This ivy-mantled folly stands back from the road, surrounded by trees. Entry is gained through the porch and the one-roomed domed interior is embellished with knucklebones and carved heads.

Many follies were designed to be more than a little intimidating. Imagine climbing through the ivy here to be welcomed by the scream of a bearded and unkempt hermit who has been especially installed to terrify visitors.

Fawley's mausoleum of the Foreman family.

Fawley Court has an eerie folly.

FINGEST

The ghost of a fourteenth-century bishop is sometimes witnessed in the woods near Fingest village. In life he was Henry Burghersh, who from 1320-1340 was Bishop of Lincoln. In those days the bishopric of Lincoln spread as far as South Buckinghamshire. Burghersh used his autonomous powers to the extreme, claiming common land for the Church. One is led to believe that Burghersh obtained a conscience posthumously, for it is his ghost (for unknown reasons dressed as a forester) that rides forever in the Fingest Woods lamenting his life of greed.

FORTY GREEN

The Royal Standard of England, the local inn, is said to have been the sheltering place of Charles II. The king was on his way to France after the Battle of Worcester in 1651. His hiding place can still be seen in the roof above the aptly named King Charles Room.

FULMER

Fulmer is reputedly haunted by the sound of a horse and cart. This invisible phantom trots its way through the tiny village. Sometimes just the clopping of a horse is heard, at other times the crunching of metal wheels on gravel is also audible.

GERRARDS CROSS

On the outskirts of the small town stands the rambling Bull. The Bull has been here since 1688 and stands on an old staging route. With the stagecoaches came the highwaymen; such a man was Jack Shrimpton, a close friend of the landlord of the Bull. It was to the Bull that Shrimpton fled when things got a bit too warm. The old inn's many sprawling rooms and twisting corridors made an ideal hideout. In all probability Shrimpton was heading for the Bull when he was arrested on the road in 1713. He was convicted and hanged at Tyburn.

Nearby Bulstrode Camp was once a vast hill fort. When William the Conqueror's troops surrounded the camp, which was occupied by the local Saxons, the Saxons refused to give up without a fight. Shobbington, the local Saxon chief, had no horses, so he and his seven brothers attacked the Normans riding wild bulls. They routed the enemy. When William heard this he summoned Shobbington to court. The Saxon arrived complete with sons and bulls. William appreciated Shobbington's boldness and let him keep his estate, which was afterwards known as Bulstrode.

GREAT MISSENDEN

Great Missenden is an attractive small town that claims to be the centre of the Chilterns and it is not short of the odd ghost story.

Missenden Abbey was founded in 1133. It is, at the time of writing, an adult education centre in the ownership of Buckinghamshire County Council. It was sold to the council in 1946 by the Carrington family; previous owners include Henry VIII, Elizabeth I and the Earl of Leicester, to whom she presented it.

It is haunted by two ladies, or one who has the option of how she dresses. The figure of a lady in a black crinoline dress has been seen on the stairway and a lady in grey Victorian attire has been witnessed by students on the staircase and also in the cloakroom. Either, or both, of these ladies have been blamed for several minor breakages, which include a vase which was thrown down the stairs and a large glass ashtray that was smashed. Forgive me for being sceptical but there is

The haunted Bull at Gerrards Cross.

Great Missenden Abbey is said to be haunted by two ghostly ladies.

nothing as boisterous or inventive as a gaggle of students, of any age; phantom ladies sound suspiciously like a convenient excuse.

Sir John de Plesser was Lord of Missenden in 1133 when the abbey was founded. He loved riding the area and was an extremely accomplished horseman. Before he died he made the monks of Missenden swear that they would bury him upright astride his great white horse. This they did and his ghost may still be seen charging across the Chiltern hillsides.

HAZLEMERE

There is a strange story here of a haunted cottage at Widmer End, which has had a history of mild poltergeist activity. Tenants would come and go in rapid succession and locals would not even walk close by the house at night. In the 1950s, one family put up a stalwart resistance and remained in the house for five years. A loud banging or rapping was heard regularly from an upstairs bedroom. However, when the bedroom door was opened, the banging ceased. Knockings were also heard on the outside door, but when the door was opened there was no one there. The family, thinking that these happenings were some type of trick performed by the villagers, set up elaborate alarms. Nobody was ever caught and even if someone had been it would not have explained some of the strange happenings. For instance, a little girl described how a small man came from behind her bedroom wardrobe and pushed his thumb deep into her back.

If there had been any village animosity towards the family one would have thought that it would have ceased with their departure in 1954. However, for the new tenants things got worse. An au pair even tried to jump out of the window when she saw the ghost of a man. Village charwomen avoided the cottage like the plague and one family of tenants found the atmosphere so overpowering that they left midway through their meal.

There is a story attached to the cottage that might have a bearing on the case. The cottage was supposedly once owned by a couple and their two sons. The man and his wife were devoted to each other. Unfortunately the wife died suddenly and the husband became a recluse, later committing suicide in the back bedroom.

HEDGERLEY

Judge Jeffreys was known throughout history for the harsh, even inhumane, treatment of those brought before him. Jeffereys' children's marriages are recorded in Hedgerley church registers. Hedgerley, however, had a more notorious and

The Shell House at Hedgerley.

sadistic law enforcer than Jeffreys. His name was Judge Ambrose Bennet. Bennet's sole purpose in life was to harass, torment and persecute the local Quakers. He would seem to have met with a certain amount of success, for many of the Quaker families moved across the Hertfordshire border out of Ambrose Bennet's jurisdiction.

I am indebted to Hilary Stainer Rice for this little story. It concerns Shell House, a seventeenth-century dwelling of character. In the 1950s Shell House was haunted by something that went bump and bounced in the attic. Apparently the noises were only heard when the space was unoccupied; they ceased when the attic was utilised as a child's bedroom. However, an overpowering atmosphere remained. There are also reports of this spirit setting off alarm clocks and making ghostly footsteps down now non-existent stairs. It has also been accused of causing a lady to drop a joint of meat, nudging guests and causing a presence on the stairs. As far as it can be ascertained nothing untoward has happened in the history of Shell House to account for this ghost.

I had heard from other sources that there is a haunting at Hedgerley Green in a sixteenth-century house, Leith Grove, which was formerly a gamekeeper's cottage. The cottage has a vague story of body snatching, a practice that was rife in the eighteenth-century. It is reported that two local men were in the trade and had their eye on an old lady at Leith Grove. The trouble was that nature was taking its time. The upshot was that they broke into the house and gave nature a shove. The old lady was murdered and her body sold to surgeons. Unsurprisingly, the inexplicable humps and bumps that spook Leith Grove are likened to the sound of a body being roughly transported. People have also experienced a drop in temperature and the aroma of rotting meat.

A young girl who stayed in the 1940s was tucked into bed by a friendly old lady. However, no one of that description was in the house at the time. Could this have been our murdered lady?

Hilary tells us of an actor friend, Leslie French, who one June was driving near Hedgerley Green when he spotted a couple of young children playing near a haystack. He waved cheerily but then realised that it was a funny time of year for a haystack. He turned and looked back, but saw nothing of the children or the haystack.

HEDSOR

Hedsor Priory, which as far as I know never actually functioned as one, sits on a hill near Bourne End. This massive construction is actually a folly built by Lord Boston. The excuse for its erection was that it was an eyecatcher – a building that obviously catches the eye and enhances the view. In this case it is a little strange, as, although the building is vast, it is inconspicuous behind a screen of high trees. People who have lived in the village for years are totally unaware of the structure. Only in 1970 was the true extent of the building revealed when some of the vegetation was removed. The building seems to float across the hillside, each turn revealing another aspect. What at first would seem to be haphazard must have been carefully planned indeed. There are three main towers, one circular, one square and one hexagonal. Nothing is over 40ft high but its placement on the hillside seems to give a feeling of great height. Looking at the ivy-covered walls and towers with their minute castellations, one would suspect that Hedsor Priory once enjoyed some purposeful function, but no. All that is known is that Lord Boston dedicated it to George III and it was probably designed by Sir William Chambers. Unfortunately there is no story here, not even a respectable ghost. It was built only to be romantic, and it works.

HIGH WYCOMBE

On the first Monday after the middle of May the Mayor of High Wycombe is weighed in and weighed out. The Chief Weights and Measures Inspector takes note of the weights of the outgoing mayor and the incoming mayor. In days gone by, if the outgoing mayor had lost weight during his year of office it was assumed that he had been lively and industrious and he was duly praised and applauded by the townsfolk. If he had gained weight it showed that he had been gluttonous and lethargic and the crowd showed their scorn by hissing and booing.

I had made up my mind not to mention UFOs in this book, as it is study of its own. It has filled many a volume and we are none of us any the wiser; it is all a matter of opinion. But the High Wycombe affair is unique because it is one of the earlier sightings and is before the early sci-fi writers such as Jules Verne and H.G. Wells. A manuscript written by William Robert Loosley, a High Wycombe undertaker, was only discovered by Loosley's great-great-granddaughter nearly 160 years after it was penned. Loosley's story begins on a warm sticky night. He was unable to sleep and at 3.15 a.m. he went to his window. He noticed a bright 'star' rapidly getting closer and, as he watched, the strange object landed nearby.

The following afternoon Loosley described the night's happenings to his family and apprentice and then proceeded to search the local terrain. He discovered a weird multi-sided metallic container about 18in in height and displaying a series of knobs and switches. As the shaken undertaker watched an 'eye' opened and a dazzling light of great strength shone out. As Loosley watched in awe various beams and rods emerged from the small metallic contraption. This was too much for Loosley and he fled, with the contraption trying to pursue. Despite his fear the undertaker noticed that the ground was crisscrossed with deep ruts. Even stranger things were to come; looking back over his shoulder

High Wycombe's robot from outer space. (*Brenda Allaway*)

Loosley watched the tiny machine grab a dead rat from the grass and rub it against a lighted side panel.

Still in flight and slowly pursued by the tiny tinny monster, Loosley lost his sense of direction and burst through some bushes into a clearing. It did nothing for the undertaker's peace of mind to discover another machine many times larger than the first. The report states that the two machines seemed to realise that they had company. The smaller machine tried to herd Loosley towards the larger one. Also, a type of moon came down from the sky and bathed the undertaker in a strange light. Loosley had had enough and fled to his home, where later he reported on seeing the small moon rise and get lost in the clouds. A strange tale: make of it what you will.

The beautiful old building known as Loakes House was built by the Marquess of Lanesbury in the seventeenth century. It is, at the time of writing, Wycombe Abbey School for Girls. The unquiet spirit here manifests itself as a horse-riding lady that once lived in the building. The unnamed lady is said to have enjoyed nothing more than a canter through the neighbouring countryside. It was in Loakes Road just near Wycombe football ground that she met her fatal accident. The horse shied and threw the rider to the ground, breaking her neck instantly. The lady's ghost is still reported to haunt the area. Early morning riders have been briefly accompanied by the spectre that disappears as suddenly as it appears.

A strange story of High Wycombe concerns dreams rather than hauntings, but it is worth a mention. A mistress at a famous public school in High Wycombe at the turn of the century was plagued by recurring dreams of her pupils being swept into a whirlpool. The young teacher informed the headmistress of her dreams. More as a precautionary measure than through any realistic fear, the headmistress enforced all her girls to take swimming lessons at the local baths. The young teacher moved abroad. In 1907, several years after the dreams, a party of some thirty girls from the school took a trip to Cookham for an afternoon of ice-skating. The ferry in which the girls were travelling overturned and sank near Bourne End. Fortunately, every girl managed to swim to safety through the freezing water. Local papers at the time reported that several of the girls stated that they owed their lives to the headmistress's forethought and the young teacher's dreams.

HUGHENDEN

Benjamin Disraeli bought Hughenden Manor when he married Wyndham Lewis's widow in 1839. He spent most of his political life at Hughenden, basking in the favours of Queen Victoria who was a frequent visitor here. Disraeli died in the house in 1881 after being raised to the peerage as Lord Beaconsfield.

Disraeli of
Hughenden Park.
(*Brenda Allaway*)

Legend dictates that the famous politician has never left the place. Much of the house has been left as it was in his heyday. Disraeli's benign ghost has often been witnessed on the upper floors of Hughenden Manor. There was also one occasion when his shade was witnessed at the bottom of the stairs with a sheath of papers in his hand.

IBSTONE

It is rumoured that some underground passages near Ibstone church hold the bodies of local gypsies. The story goes that two feuding families did battle on a nearby common. Several gypsies died in the conflict but the local authorities refused to accept the expense of burying them. The problem was reputedly solved by placing the bodies in the underground tunnels. Personally I doubt this story. Having associated closely with our Romany friends for over fifty years I cannot ever imagine them showing such irreverence to the dead.

35

IVER HEATH

For the following story I am indebted to Mr Barham, who describes how, in 1972, a young lady was driven away from a party near Slough. She was taken to a clearing in a wood where some type of occult ceremony was being enacted. This involved people wearing animal masks and performing various animated actions. The lady was returned unharmed but could not obtain an explanation. Black Park at Iver Heath was thought to be the venue of this unusual occurrence.

LANE END

The spirit of the Lady in Red haunts the footpaths near the hamlet of Lane End. Towards the end of the nineteenth century, a village girl named Anna was preparing for her forthcoming wedding. Anna was a village beauty who always favoured dresses of deep red. She worked as a barmaid at the alehouse in the nearby village of Wheelerend Common. It was at the inn she met her beau, a handsome young labourer who worked at Muswell Farm near Hanover Hill. All went well until ten days before the wedding when poor Anna was struck down by an unknown illness. In spite of the endeavours of local practitioners Anna expired.

Shortly after her death the spirit of a lady in a maroon velvet dress was witnessed crossing the fields at Lane End. The law of probability persuaded witnesses that this was the lovely Anna, her unquiet spirit trying vainly to make the appointment she so sadly missed in life.

Anna would seem to have been one of the most active of spirits, appearing no less than thirty times in one particular year. However, time was perhaps a great healer for nothing was seen of the forlorn maid after the 1940s. That is until some quarter of a century had elapsed, for in the mid-'60s a phantom lady dressed in a wine-red dress was witnessed climbing Hanover Hill. What could cause a slight change of venue? Could Anna's bereft spirit have tired of waiting for her beau at the appointed meeting place and now be searching for him near his place of employment?

LANGLEY

The stately home of Ditton Park was once one of the country seats of the Duke of Buccleugh. A story tells that when the old place was undergoing some extensive rebuilding, some church plate was found in a wall. The finding implied that there had been a chapel in the house. This discovery by itself was of little significance

Lane End has a haunting Lady in Red.

until a short time later, when one of the gardeners noticed a funeral procession making its way across the lawn. The figures were distinct and by their attire it was evident that they came from mediaeval times. The gardener watched dumbfounded as the figures meandered towards him. The procession halted and then vanished as quickly as it had appeared. The gardener had the presence of mind to mark the spot. Ensuing excavations proved the patch of ground to be the site of an ancient chapel.

Another large house in Langley went by the romantic name of Love Hill. The house experienced some poltergeist activity in the 1850s. A violent, uncanny argument was often heard and books were thrown as if in temper. Love Hill's owner, Sir Frederick Ouseley, also saw the manifestations of a gentleman in a bright yellow coat. He described his spectral visitor as having a rough face and extremely piercing eyes. Investigations finally traced the haunting quarrelling voices to a spare room on the ground floor. The floorboards were lifted and the skeletons of a woman and child revealed. The remains were given a Christian burial and the hauntings came to an end.

For a more recent Langley haunting in a far more humble abode I am indebted to Angus MacNaghten. The story concerns some almshouses near Langley church. An old inhabitant of the houses, Mrs Briggs, was a little disturbed when some of the dwellings were used to accommodate evacuated children during the Second World War. She stated that the almshouses were intended for the use of villagers and that she would not rest until they were returned to their original purpose. Unfortunately, Mrs Briggs died before such an event took place. After her death she proceeded to haunt the properties, manifesting herself in a house that was being rented by a young couple. Not only did the old lady make a personal appearance but she was also blamed for all sorts of poltergeist activity. Crockery was broken, a heavy bookcase was moved and covers were pulled from beds. Life became intolerable for the residents. A cleric was called in and an exorcism took place. No more phenomena occurred and old Mrs Briggs would seem to be at peace.

LITTLE MARLOW

I am indebted to John J. Eddleston for some of the following facts concerning George Arthur Bailey. George Arthur Bailey considered himself some type of entrepreneur. He boasted of discovering a new notation for musical scores. This was George's reason, or rather excuse, for advertising for young ladies to come and learn of his ideas on music that would sweep the country.

Police were already showing some interest in Bailey and his abode at Little Marlow, Buckinghamshire. It would seem that he was more discerning about the personal attractiveness of his would-be lady students than their capacity for learning. When receiving a reply from Gladys Millicent Edwards, Bailey wrote back saying that he wanted 'smart, exceptionally attractive persons, of height, preferably full build'. What this conceivably had to do with accomplishing his new musical ideas one is left to wonder.

On 29 September 1920 Gladys Edwards had been joined for a lecture at Barn Cottage by two other smart young ladies, Lillian Marks and a Miss Field. After the day's studying was done, Bailey dismissed the girls but requested Miss Marks to return that evening for extra tuition.

On 30 September when the other two girls had turned up at the appointed time they remarked on Miss Mark's absence. They were simply told that she had gone out.

On 2 October Lillian Marks made a complaint about Bailey. She informed the police that she worked late on 29 September and had been persuaded to stay the night in the spare room. Later Bailey had attempted to rape her, without success.

In the meantime Gladys Edwards had been invited back for extra evening tutorials but had been lucky enough to find the place in darkness. Barn Cottage was searched and the body of Kate Bailey, George's wife, was found in the front bedroom. She had been poisoned. A post-mortem also revealed that she was pregnant. Bailey swore that she had taken the poison herself. Also, that he had approached Miss Marks that evening not with the idea of sexual assault on his mind but just to make sure she did not wander about and discover the body of a suicide. The police were unconvinced by his story. Why should an innocent man even give a lecture with his wife dead upstairs, let alone persuade a young lady to stay the night in such circumstances? At his trial at Aylesbury, Bailey's story was obviously full of holes. As if that was not condemning enough, it was revealed that he had told an even less likely story to his brother-in-law, William Jennings. Jennings was told that his sister had gone to Wycombe Hospital for a premature birth and had died. The jury, which incidentally contained for the first time female members, brought the inevitable verdict of guilty.

George Arthur Bailey was hanged at Oxford on Wednesday 2 March 1921; he was twenty-two years old. The hangman was John Ellis and his assistant was Edward Taylor.

Little Marlow is reputed to possess at least a couple of ghosts. The most famous is a lady that stands in the road causing motorists to have accidents. Sometimes it is just a figure, gender unknown, and as drivers swerve to miss it the figure disappears. A WI member from Little Marlow (*The Buckingham Village Book*) claims she clearly witnessed an auburn-haired woman in her bedroom. The writer describes in detail the lady's long-sleeved turquoise nightdress. The lady was holding a cup and appeared to be puzzled or lost. She then turned and disappeared through a closed door. Whether or not this is the spectral lady jaywalker is open to conjecture.

Little Marlow – an attractive village with a horrific secret.

LITTLE MISSENDEN

The Little Abbey Hotel is just yards from the main abbey building. It is supposedly connected by a subterranean tunnel, the use of which was to allow the Augustine monks from the abbey to visit the nuns at the small building to provide Sacrament. I am led to believe that one of their numerous vows forbade them from leaving the abbey. The passageway was discovered in a period when the Little Abbey was functioning as a local school.

The monks of Missenden were at one stage known as the Black Monks, because of their attire. It is strange therefore that the spectre of the Little Abbey Hotel is clothed in a brown hood and cassock. The apparition made so many appearances during the 1950s that the hotel staff refused to go into one particular lounge.

A descriptive report was made in 1972 by a workman employed by the hotel. He describes how he was fixing a window on a landing when a brown-cassocked monk ascended the stairs. The workman politely stood aside to let the brother pass; he seemed deep in meditation with his hands together as if in prayer. The handyman did not notice which way the monk turned but later found all three possible exit rooms locked with their keys in the hotel foyer. There has been much speculation as to who the ghostly brother is. He is thought by some to be a monk who committed suicide rather than face discipline for a misdemeanour. The main trouble with this theory is that the only record of a suicide is that of a novice nun in 1297. Whoever or whatever the spectre is, it is certainly not of female gender.

Another better-known candidate for the spectre is Roger Palmer, an incumbent of the abbey. In 1530 Palmer was witnessed, dressed only in doublet and hose and with a sheathed sword, leaving the premises of a married woman. It is assumed that Roger had been 'a rogering'. Palmer's promiscuous behaviour brought about a scandal that finally closed the abbey. Is it possible that the praying spectral monk is Roger Palmer, guilt ridden by the fact that such a brief moment of carnal pleasure should have such dire consequences?

Recently I searched for Little Missenden Abbey; I visited it years ago but villagers now deny its existence. Could it have disappeared when the new dual carriageway came along, or could it now be enclosed in the larger abbey grounds? Please write and let me know.

MARLOW

The prodigious relic, the hand of St James of Compostela, is kept in the small Catholic church of St Peter at Marlow. This relic was of the utmost importance during the Middle Ages and people would make pilgrimages to Reading Abbey where the hand was originally displayed.

The hand was said to have healing powers and a mediaeval manuscript dated from the twelfth century is said to list no less than twenty-eight healing miracles attributed to the hand. Apparently it was a simple process to dip the hand in holy water and then sprinkle the water on the affected part of the body. The earliest recorded miracle relates to 1156 when the Sheriff of Surrey, Mauger Malcuvenant, was on the point of death. He was revived by a few drops of holy water that had been sprinkled over the hand. In the heyday of St James's hand, devout pilgrims would gather in Reading before taking the arduous trip to St James's shrine at Compostela, Spain.

Windsor bargees on the River Thames were not the most highly principled of men. A cook at Eton noticed that food was readily disappearing from her larder. To pay back the thieves she took some puppies that had recently been

Marlow Bridge, where the bargees enjoyed puppy dog pie.

Marlow's spotted boy. (*Brenda Allaway*)

put down and baked them into a pie. Sure enough the pie disappeared. However, the following day much of the pie was found discarded on the river bank under Marlow Bridge. Apparently the bargees had not found the pie as appetising as usual. They were never to live it down and for many years Eton schoolboys would scream across the river to the bargees questioning, 'Who ate puppy pie under Marlow Bridge?'

In the 1830s Marlow was the home of John Richardson, the entrepreneur and showman. Richardson had risen from the workhouse to become a wealthy impresario of worldwide fame. His speciality was freaks and he searched the world for his performers.

When Richardson performed before Queen Victoria at Windsor one of the star acts was a 'spotted boy'. The showman had found the four-year-old in the West Indies and claimed he had saved him from a life of poverty. This claim was probably true; freaks did not have a bad life at all. They were well cared for, even pampered. The boy, who suffered from an unusual disease that brought his dark skin out in large pink blotches, was a special favourite of Richardson, who named him George Alexander Gratton. The showman was heartbroken when George died, aged five years old, and had him interred, only to be exhumed and reburied with him many years later.

A ghostly lady was seen crossing fields near Marlow's Seymour House.

A ghost that is still quite regularly witnessed is the Grey Lady of Seymour Court. The old Seymour Court that was in the greater part destroyed during the Civil War was originally the home of Jane Seymour. The present building is far more recent. The Grey Lady has been seen at regular intervals for many years. But Hilary Stainer Rice gives the most lucid account, sent to her by a correspondent. The writer states that as a boy, during the Second World War, he lived in a wooden abode a stone's throw from Seymour Court. As with many other families in the country, the writer's parents had constructed a small air-raid shelter. In this case the family had dug deep into the side of a hill. After spending a night in his makeshift necessity the boy awoke one morning to find the rest of the family had returned to the house. On his way home the boy noticed a lady dressed in grey walking towards him. She seemed unaware of his presence. Being shy, the boy hid behind a tree from where he took mental note of the lady's apparel. She was in her mid-twenties and wore a cloak with a hood from which black curly hair emerged from the fringe. The lady made her way past the secret observer and headed towards Seymour Court. She did not disappear until she turned a corner by some bushes. What is remarkable about the case is that the lady was so lifelike the boy took her to be a guest at the house and later enquired about the visitor.

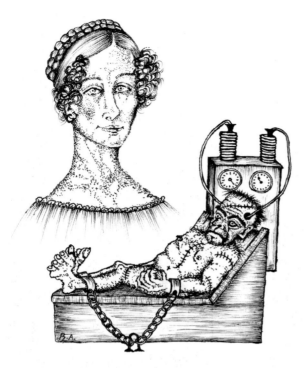

Mary Shelley, wife of Percy Bysshe, created *Frankenstein* at Marlow. *(Brenda Allaway)*

He was told that there were no guests that week. He had witnessed the famous Grey Lady of Seymour Court.

Another famous Marlow resident was Mary Shelley. Although Mary published several works, she will always be remembered for *Frankenstein*. The book, reputed to be the first horror story, was written by Mary in 1818 whilst staying at Lake Geneva with her new husband Percy Bysshe and his friend Lord Byron. Byron suggested a writing competition, Mary gladly accepted and produced arguably the worlds greatest horror story of all time.

MEDMENHAM

The original Medmenham Abbey was erected by Hugh de Bolebec in 1210. It is said that the worthy gentleman did it as a penance for his sins. Shortly after, it was opened to the Cistercian monks.

Behind the monks' holy and moralistic exterior, unruly, unrestrained and even unlawful activity often took place. One of the earliest felonies was recorded in 1312. The Abbot of Medmenham was accused of forcibly entering the Manor of Dunrugge, felling the trees and purloining the timber.

John Wilkes, one of the
revellers at Medmenham
Abbey.

In the sixteenth century came the dissolution of the monasteries. Medmenham
Abbey was stripped of anything useful and all manner of metals were stolen and
transformed into Henry's guns and other weapons.

Reconstructed by James Duffield at the turn of the seventeenth century, the
abbey became a private family home. Several centuries later a descendant of James,
Francis Duffield, made the acquaintance of the notorious Francis Dashwood. The
stories of Dashwood and his Brotherhood of St Francis are world famous and too
numerous to be detailed here. Suffice it to say that Dashwood immediately saw
Medmenham Abbey as an ideal residence for the Brotherhood. The infamous
Dashwood seemed to have a hold over Duffield and it was not long before the
building had been transformed. A 'ruined' tower was added and the house was

greatly enlarged; sordid and pornographic paintings began to adorn the walls, inanimate witnesses of the manifest debauchery. The gardens now included nooks, crannies, small caves, bowers and grottos. Hidden alcoves emerged where rampant 'brothers' entrapped giggling nuns. Lechery, hard-drinking, depravity, perversion and excess wantonness were the order of the day.

Unfortunately for Sir Francis, the activities described above could not remain a secret in such a tiny hamlet as Medmenham. The notorious goings-on soon attracted a host of spectators. Dashwood reluctantly moved the Brotherhood to his caves at West Wycombe. Here the debauchery continued, and increased, but at a venue a lot more sheltered from the prying eyes of the curious. (I am indebted to Tony Barham's *Witchcraft in the Thames Valley* for this little story of Medmenham.)

As suggested above, the notorious Sir Francis Dashwood made the village a tourist hotspot in Victorian times. A schoolmaster from Reading arrived by boat with many others and as he stepped ashore he was dismayed to find how commercialised the site had become. He was greeted by a nine-year-old gypsy girl who escorted him to the Windmill Inn (no longer in existence). With other tourists he was then taken to see Bullbank Castle earthworks. The whistle-stop tour then took in the Hemming Well, after refusing a two-mile trip to Hollowick. At Hemming Well an ancient crone, the nine-year-old's grandmother, related some blood-curdling and most improbable stories. After paying their dues, the company made for the Dog and Badger, exhausted by a tour that had obviously been designed to drain and jade them and make them keen to pay off their energetic escort.

One of the most notorious episodes concerning the Brotherhood of St Francis took place at Medmenham Abbey. The aforementioned Sir Francis Dashwood had surrounded himself with the brotherhood one night. They stood in the ring trying to call up the Devil. Some of the land's greatest gentry chanted verbal tommy-rot as ordered by Dashwood. All of a sudden the Devil, complete with red attire, horns and tail, bounded into the room, landing on Lord Sandwich's shoulders. The distinguished lord took flight, screaming, 'Spare me gracious Devil.' It was a source of amusement for months, after it was realised that it was just a pet ape, dressed as Satan who had been released by a servant at Sir Francis' signal.

A mile and a half outside the village is the splendorous Danefield House Hotel. I cannot think of another half-dozen hotels in the country with such a perfect setting mixed with such grandiose rooms affording such delightful prospects. Seen from the Thames in its true magnificence one feels obliged to draw parallels with romantic castles on the Rhine.

I could discover little of the ghost which is reported to roam one of the corridors. Danefield House is the third building on the site and is the manifestation of a soap millionaire's dream. Robert Hudson indulged in this extravagance at the end of the nineteenth century. It is rumoured that even *his* wealth was not limitless and he had to sell the mansion shortly after completion to cover his expenses.

After a few fruitless enquiries concerning the ghost I gave up and just enjoyed the ambience for a brief half an hour. I should like to be able to tell the reader that the obscure ghost is Robert Hudson regretting his speedy departure from his Thameside utopia. Unfortunately there is no evidence to support this, and the ghost, if there is a ghost, is probably more at home with one of the earlier dwellings on the site.

PENN

Penn stands 600ft up amongst the beech woods. Villagers once boasted that from the lofty church tower they could see a dozen counties.

The Penns, after whom the village was named, were here from at least the sixteenth century. One of the family, William Penn (1644-1718), a Quaker, made his mark across the Atlantic and is commemorated by the state of Pennsylvania in the USA.

An eighteenth-century labourer on a horse haunts the countryside around Penn. People have heard the approach of galloping hooves but turned to see nothing. Others have watched a horseman coming towards them through the mist, but when he's a couple of yards from them he bursts into an upsetting peel of maniacal laughter and then promptly disappears.

PRESTWOOD

There is a corner in Prestwood where dogs and horses stubbornly refuse to pass after nightfall. However, a spiritual horse seems less timid than its earthbound brothers. The rider of this pure white spectral stallion is a lady holding her head in her hands. How she navigates with her particular predicament is unknown, but she always follows the same path up to Stony Green Hall.

There is also an earthbound spirit that wanders near Moat Farm. The unhappy ghost is thought to be an ex-farm tenant searching for a cache of gold and guineas that he secreted in the wall of the building many years ago. The spirit will have an endless and fruitless search; his hoard was discovered by builders who were altering the premises many years ago.

SPEEN

Rumour has it that a highwayman named Cooper haunts Highwood Bottom, apparently keeping an eye on his buried treasure. It is difficult to ascertain if it is the highwayman, his hoard or both that lies under the stone in the vicinity. It is most surprising that the authorities have not raised the stone to discover what is hidden underneath. A private expedition of local boys attempted such a feat some time ago. However, their courage deserted them and they fled, obviously none the wiser.

STOKE POGES

> The curfew tolls the knell of parting day,
> The lowing herd wind slowly o'er the lea,
> The plowman homeward plods his weary way,
> And leaves the world to darkness and to me.

Arguably the most famous verse in English poetry; it is of course the opening lines of Gray's 'Elegy Written in a Country Churchyard'. The churchyard in question is that at Stoke Poges.

Thomas Gray (1716-1771) was the sole survivor of his parent's twelve children. An inheritance from his father permitted him to go to Cambridge and study law. Gray later bought his mother a house at Stoke Poges where he visited her on holiday, and it was here that he penned his most famous work.

Gray is buried beside his mother at the church and close by is a huge sarcophagus erected by John Penn and dedicated to Gray. John Penn, grandson of William Penn of Pennsylvania, also constructed the vast Palladian country house which is now Stoke Poges Golf Club. This was part of the set for *Goldfinger* and one of the statues in the grounds was once decapitated by Oddjob's bowler hat.

STONEY GREEN

I first alighted on the following story in Andrew Green's *Our Haunted Kingdom*, the ghost hunters' Bible. This is another haunting horsewoman who is seen riding at Bryants Bottom near Stoney Green. She has seldom, if ever, been witnessed since the early 1960s. Reputed to be the 'Lady of the Manor', she galloped off at high speed after being accused of infidelity by her husband. Whether she was guilty or not will never be known. It is thought that her temper overtook her horsemanship skills and she was thrown from the horse and died of a broken neck.

Monumental gardens
at Stoke Poges.

John Penn's vast
and rather eccentric
monument to a rather
eccentric genius.

TAPLOW

Back in Norman times, Hitcham Manor, near Taplow, was inhabited by two brothers called de Crispin. All went well until they both fell in love with the same lady, a daughter of the famous Lord of Dorney.

The lady, in the fullness of time, married one of the brothers but unfortunately for him she continued to bestow her affections on the other. Returning early one day, brother one discovered brother two *flagrante delicto* with his wife. In a fit of jealous rage he murdered the lady. His penance for such a deed was that he was ordered to make a pilgrimage to the Holy Land. This he did, but he returned unrepentant. This was unacceptable to the authorities so they laid a curse upon him that he and his descendants would never die peacefully. The legend has existed since that day that the bloody handprint of the murdered lady appears on the family coat of arms just before a de Crispin meets his maker.

A white witch from nearby Cippenham was famous for her knowledge of herbs. She was reported to be hideously ugly but never to cause trouble by casting spells or making curses. It was reported that Walter de la Mare, who lived at Taplow, befriended her and placed her in several of his short stories.

TURVILLE

'The sleeping maid of Turville' is a difficult story to get to grips with. It probably dates back to the 1870s and therefore is nearly impossible to study. Tony Barham's *Witchcraft in the Thames Valley* makes a valiant effort to produce a plausible tale, a preécis of which follows.

Mrs Sadler was a widow living with her daughter in the village of Turville. Mrs Sadler is described as being large, cheerful, if possibly a little bossy and her daughter is described as caring and dreamy. On leaving the house one morning, when she was just thirteen, the daughter complained of feeling faint. She returned in the evening and went to bed, but could not be awakened the following morning.

Despite calls from the neighbours, a physician and the much regarded vicar, the young lady could not be awakened. Weeks turned into months, the maid slept on. Her fame spread and people travelled vast distances to witness Turville's Sleeping Maid. Widow Sadler was experiencing a not unpleasant change of circumstances as appreciative people pushed money into her hand on leaving. Soon the story, spread by the newspapers and verified by well-respected scientists, was known all over the country. Mrs Sadler, along with local shopkeepers and publicans, celebrated an ever increasing fortune, as Turville was now the place to be seen, a euphoria peaking with a visit from the Prince of Wales.

Doubt of course was inevitable. Opium was suspected but never proved. Experts searched the cottage, sniffing for the drug's unusual aroma. Discussions and arguments filled the news sheets; all opinions though came to nothing.

In early 1880 there was a hue and cry through the streets one particular morning when it was discovered that widow Sadler had died. She had fallen down the stairs and broken her neck. There was then some controversy of what to do with the sleeping maid. At Christmas time in 1880, after nearly ten years of slumber, it was decided to move her to a nearby neighbour's cottage. On that cold morning, as she was being stretchered the short distance, the maid stirred and flickered her eyes. Shortly after she was wide awake and seemingly none the worse for wear following her long ordeal.

The young lady remained in the village for just a few more days, staying with a neighbour. She then left Turville never to return. Gossip has it that she moved to Reading, where she married and raised a large family.

It is unusual for such a small village as Turville to have two intriguing mysteries, but such is the case. Not far from the village's black-capped windmill stands the village church, almost unique due to its fifteenth-century flint tower. The surprising possession beneath the tower is a massive stone coffin hewn from

Turville church, home of the mysterious massive stone coffin.

a single stone. The coffin was known to contain the body of a thirteenth-century priest. However, it was opened in living memory and found to have lost its original inhabitant, who had been replaced with a woman's skeleton.

Experts decided that the exchange had been made as early as the fourteenth century. A second surprise was that the woman had apparently been murdered – examination of the bones revealed the mark of a bullet. It will never be known what sad tragedy led to the lady's demise, or why it was necessary to hide her remains or what happened to the exhumed priest.

WEST WYCOMBE

There have been literally volumes relating to the history of Sir Francis Dashwood and his notorious Hellfire Club. So much has been written that I have very little if anything to add. Therefore I shall be brief.

The Hellfire Club originally manifested in nearby Medmenham but later moved to West Wycombe. The membership, that included Dashwood and John Wilkes, also attracted its members from some of the foremost families in the land. Lord Sandwich, first Lord Mayor of the Admiralty, was a member, as was George Bubb Doddington, the Baron of Melcome Regis and Thomas Potter, son of the Archbishop of Canterbury. There was also the Earl of March and numerous others, all with the aim of shocking and disgusting the people of England with blatant wickedness.

West Wycombe was good for such a sect, but alterations had to be made. The Church of St Lawrence, said to be built on an Iron Age site, was altered by Dashwood. He added a great gold-encased finial; the ball could be seen for miles and could accommodate up to nine men. Below the church Sir Francis excavated caves for his orgies of devil worship and black magic. The excavated chalk was used to lay a road to High Wycombe. A pedestal with a round ball on top marks Dashwood's achievement. Between 1763 and 1765, at the head of the caves Dashwood employed John Bastard to build an eight-sided mausoleum. In itself this roofless hexagonal gives an aspect of forbidding mystery. The grounds were not to be ignored. Wherever anything outrageous could cause the maximum feelings of shock and horror there, it was constructed. It is said that the grounds were designed to assimilate the body of a naked woman with a cave entrance appropriately placed. Also trees were planted in patterns of great vulgarity.

Next Dashwood added the temples: the Four Winds, Daphne's, Flora's, Bacchus and the Music Temple, each surpassing the other with the exotic and the erotic. John Wilkes, a regular visitor here, found one lewd above all others.

In 1763, when some members were ageing and beginning to worry a little about their sins in the afterlife, membership began to dwindle. In answer to this, Dashwood tried to encourage new clients with more bizarre attractions. One keen new member was Paul Whitehead, who some say lived in one of the small caves as a hermit. When he died, as was his request, Dashwood received his extracted heart. Unfortunately, this little treasure seems to have been lost.

Today one may walk around the estate and down to the caves at leisure. They are as gloomy and overpowering as ever, despite a running commentary and painted plaster figures. The place deserves to be haunted and is, although only irregularly.

One ghost is really more of a strange occurrence from time to time; red fingers appear on a tablet erected in the church to Dashwood. I can find out little more.

The ghost of a whimpering man that haunts the grounds is thought to be the spirit of Paul Whitehead and a sobbing woman in blue could well be the ghost of Sukie, a lady from a tavern in the town, whose story I shall unashamedly report verbatim from my *Haunted Inns of the Chilterns and Thames Valley* published in 1993.

Near the centre of the village is the tall, gaunt George and Dragon. The inn was a staging post for the London to Oxford mail and during the Dashwood era was already over 300 years old. In 1720 a renovation took place and the inn was given the uniformly accepted façade of a flat brick frontage. At this time the famous massive lead sign was added with a colourful illustration of St George slaying the dragon. The inn has had a number of spiritual manifestations, the majority of which are obscure and seldom witnessed.

The first one, yet another nun, this time dressed in white, has been occasionally witnessed in the garden. The lady's pedigree is unknown but there is speculation that she is one of Dashwood's friends from Medmenham Abbey. Several ladies were thought to have disappeared during the Hellfire days but this is once again merely conjecture, an idea supposedly substantiated by the rumour of a tunnel from the George and Dragon to the caves.

The White Nun is one of a quartet of lady spirits at the inn. Another is a benign and inoffensive lady who has been witnessed by several landladies, sitting in a parlour chair. Yet another (possibly Sukie – who we will talk of later – but possibly not) appears in a white dress. She is a little frightening as the spirit appears at the foot of the bed of some poor guest and 'balloons out at you'. These are the words of an American visitor named Robbins who was unfortunate enough to encounter the lady whilst staying at the hotel in 1966. He goes on to qualify the statement by likening the apparition to a face reflected in a rounded shiny surface. A similar effect may be encountered by watching one's own face in the reflection of a shiny metal ball swinging first towards one and then away. The American gentleman was quite badly affected by the experience.

The George and Dragon at West Wycombe, home of the ghostly Sukie.

Apart from the spirits mentioned above there has also been footsteps on the stairs and some mild poltergeist activity. The activity has been relatively harmless, just the misplacing of certain domestic articles. The gender of these two spirits is unknown, but the moving of articles seems to have the touch of a woman about it.

Then of course there is Sukie (Susan). Sukie is the most famous of all the George and Dragon's manifestations. It has been suggested that she is responsible for all the naughtiness mentioned above and also that she is the composite of all three female apparitions. This is highly unlikely, especially in the case of the supposedly celibate Sister.

Sukie has a colourful story to tell dating back to the 1770s. She worked as a barmaid at the St George and Dragon at the time when Dashwood had recently completed his caves. She was very attractive and knew it, using her comeliness to evoke favours from the local lads and farmers. There was always someone about to offer a small present for a sexual encounter. Whereas Sukie was not exactly a prostitute, full or part time, she was an extremely enthusiastic amateur who was not adverse to the odd gratuity.

With the coming of the Hellfire Club there also came affluence, in the form of London visitors. Gentlemen in fine clothes and ladies in silks and satins bedecked with jewellery were now staying at the inn, rather than having a fleeting visit whilst the horses were changed on a journey to London or Oxford.

Sukie became ambitious and set her sights on the wealthy young bucks who were visiting, rather than the village louts. She began to be a little selective, denying the locals her favours and saving herself for the more promising of the visitors. Sukie was not a fool, she knew her looks were a finite asset and would swiftly forsake her; she wanted a husband, preferably a rich one.

A young man did come into the amorous barmaid's life about this time: an affluent young man, a friend and guest of Sir Francis Dashwood. A man who made a lot of promises in bed. A plausible young gentleman, so much so that Sukie's favours became his and his alone, to the exclusion of all others. Unfortunately, Sukie's monogamous sex life was not at all welcomed by the lads of the village. Since the arrival of her intended, they had been forced into a way of life verging on the celibate. Sukie was getting ideas above her station; Sukie would have to be taught a lesson. An ingenious plan was hatched.

One of the lads had struck up an acquaintance with a scholar in High Wycombe and this gave him the opportunity of getting the young man to write a letter to Sukie purporting to be from her lover. The gist of the letter was that he would be going abroad shortly and wanted to marry her before he went. He would be passing through West Wycombe late that night and would meet her in the Hellfire Caves with a preacher and witnesses to perform the ceremony.

On receiving the letter Sukie was over the moon. The hours passed by slowly as she sat in her room at the inn. Evening finally came, a fine drizzle descended. Sukie, adorned in a long white wedding dress, set out from the George and Dragon across the park. The fine drizzle had wetted the grass and Sukie's long dress was mud-stained and her hair dishevelled as she panted up the steep incline to the entrance of the caves. She finally made it, disordered and untidy but extremely ardent. She got a torch from the cave entrance and took some trouble lighting it with a flint. This accomplished, she descended the labyrinth of passages down to the main chamber. Imagine the dark tunnels, the small ineffective light and the young maid periodically calling the name of her lover. As she reached a smaller chamber about midway to her destination, she passed a large rock. As she did so an unseen hand grabbed her torch and dashed it out. Unearthly screams and hideous shrieks terrified the young maid as the three young lads jumped around her screeching at the top of their voices.

Panic-stricken and disorientated, Sukie fled in the darkness. Ribald giggles and hysterical laughter followed her as the youths celebrated the success of their scheme. But tragedy was to follow; Sukie, fleeing in the darkness, tripped over a rock on the uneven floor, dashing her head against the wall of the cave. She lay there motionless as the three lads stared in disbelief. What had started as a silly game had ended in tragedy; Sukie was alive but comatose. One of the lads ran to the village to obtain help. Villagers returned with a makeshift stretcher and bore the luckless maid down to the George and Dragon. Sukie died there in her room in the small hours of the morning. A tragic tale indeed.

Sukie's restless spirit was soon on the scene. The two maids that shared her room at the George and Dragon swore they had had a visitation from their lost colleague only days after the unhappy event. Both steadfastly refused to enter the room again.

Since then, Sukie has made regular visits to the inn. In the 230-odd years since the tragedy there have been countless sightings, some as recent as the 1980s. Poor Sukie – will she ever rest, or will she forever search for a husband amongst the customers of the George and Dragon? Most reports of her apparition seem to be in the bedrooms of male guests. Perhaps she feels more at home in these situations?

2

CENTRAL BUCKINGHAMSHIRE

ASTON CLINTON

Aston Clinton is a small and attractive village situated on Akeman Street, a well-known Roman road. Not far from this wild tract of Roman thoroughfare lies Vache's Farm. Here the apparition of a man in an old-fashioned brown frockcoat has been witnessed on several occasions. The identity of this gentleman is unknown. What is unusual, and worthy of note, is that this visitation was once witnessed by three persons simultaneously.

Near Aston Clinton, on the side of the Chilterns, lies Faithful's grave. The trouble is that now nobody knows quite where. Faithful was a shepherd and so loved a particular patch of hillside that he asked his colleagues to bury him there. After his death his fellow shepherds complied with his wishes. For good measure they cut the following into the turf:

> Faithful lived and faithful died,
> Faithful shepherd on the hillside,
> The field so high, the hill so round,
> In the day of judgement he'll be found.

For some time after his death local villagers kept the letters in clear and fine condition. But those of Faithful's age finally died off and the grave was left unattended. The grave, however, was still respected by the local populace, but not so by the local farmer, who ploughed the ground over.

ASTON SANDFORD

The ghost of a former nineteenth-century vicar and diarist, Revd Thomas Scott, makes periodic visits to the local church. The reverend prefers to call slightly before evensong; he stands beside the pulpit and overseas the preliminary proceedings. A witness stated that the apparition remains for about three

The spectral Revd Thomas Scott keeps an eye on the church at Aston Sandford. *(Brenda Allaway)*

minutes before fading away. Obviously the devout churchman shows as much interest posthumously as he did during his days of occupation. The Revd Scott would seem to be well contented with the present administration as his periodic visitations are becoming far fewer.

AYLESBURY

For an old and colourful town, Aylesbury seems to have very little in the way of ghosts. There is, however, a story of a phantom dog on the outskirts of the town. A farmer going to milk his cows each morning found his way blocked by a large black dog with fiery eyes. The menacing canine regularly sat by a gap in the hedge the farmer used as a shortcut.

Being put out by these circumstances, the farmer and a friend decided to drive the beast away. On their next meeting the farmer raised his heavy milk yoke above his head and brought it down with considerable force upon the animal. At that instant the dog disappeared and the yoke descended onto the hard ground. The farmer fell unconscious and was paralysed for the remainder of his life.

It is amazing how history and legend idolises and romanticises some people and totally neglects others. A case in point is Dick Turpin, a cowardly lying blaggard and a torturer of women. Dick could not ride well. The fictitious and quite impossible ride to York was the invention of Ainsworth in a novel – he never intended it to be taken as factual. Turpin was a poor shot. Tom King might have lived but Black Bess is an invention of the novelist's fertile mind.

Dick's spirit is the most overworked of all ghosts. It has been witnessed in nearly 200 pubs, many in areas he never visited whilst on this mortal coil. If you want a true romantic highwayman who was associated with Aylesbury, and who was an expert horseman, try Richard Ferguson, known as Galloping Dick.

Dick was born in Hertfordshire, the son of a gentleman's gentleman, and frequently travelled to London and fashionable Bath. Dick was sent to a good school but his non-appreciation of learning and his wayward disposition was not conducive with the disciplined regime. His father withdrew him and found him employment as a stable boy. Soon after, the postilion fell ill and Dick temporarily took the position. He was somewhat disenchanted, however, when the man recovered and he was reinstated as the lowly stable boy. With the help of his father, Dick soon regained his position of postilion with a lady of high station. There was a certain charm and charisma about young Ferguson which made him extremely popular with the ladies. This was to be his downfall; his mistress caught him in a compromising position with her maid and dismissed him.

Ferguson had gathered around him a gang of lethargic layabouts and it was his known association with them and his insolent manner that lost him several good positions.

We next hear of Dick being employed by a family in Piccadilly. Shortly after, his father died, leaving him a substantial inheritance. This permitted Dick to live like a gentleman for a limited time. At Drury Lane one night he engaged in conversation with a lady named Nancy and returned with her to her abode. Ferguson became infatuated with her, which was another mistake. Firstly, Nancy thought him to be wealthy, and secondly she was acquainted with several highwaymen, a fact that she kept well hidden from her ardent admirer. Our hero's small fortune was quickly disappearing on the insatiable Nancy so he found it necessary to find employment, again as a postilion.

The coach on which Ferguson was employed was held up by a man named Abershaw. Unfortunately for both, a quick breeze blew up the robber's mask and Dick recognised the man, who was a frequent guest of Nancy. Abershaw and his colleagues waited for Ferguson at an inn where they bought his silence. Dick thankfully received the money and made for his beloved Nancy. He was not well received; she had learned of his lowly financial situation and refused him entry.

Dick turned to the bottle; here fate played another hand. Drinking at an inn one night he fell in with Abershaw and his cronies. They seemed to have money to burn and it was not long before Ferguson agreed to join them. However, rather than being directly involved, Abershaw thought his new young recruit would be better employed by remaining at the inn where he worked and informing the gang when one of the more affluent clientele took to the road. The plan worked well. Ferguson made a lot of money that was always destined for debauchery. The innkeeper, however, became suspicious and sacked him. This made Dick of little use to Abershaw, so he took to the road on his own. For several years he successfully plagued Maidenhead Thicket, Hampstead Heath and the Edgware Road. It was at the Edgware Road where Dick escaped through sheer speed and excellent horsemanship. His companions were caught, tried and hanged. Now known as Galloping Dick he used his horsemanship skills as an alibi. On the several occasions he was arrested it was thought impossible that he could commit a crime and then be witnessed 40 miles away a couple of hours later and so he was released.

Dick's luck ran out at Aylesbury when his horse went lame after a highway robbery. However, he still managed to escape, but was arrested a couple of days later at Bow Street. Aylesbury had a prior claim on Ferguson and he was conveyed in chains to that town where he met his fate with brave resignation.

Charles White from East Woodhay, down in Hampshire, was proud of his massive family. Every one of his dozen or more children were accomplished rustlers and horse thieves. Add to this a dozen or so uncles and cousins and the Whites, headed by Charles, were formidable indeed.

Sadly for Charles his force was somewhat depleted when four of his sons were hanged at Aylesbury. Charles and some more of his sons had decided to spring the four with a plan that involved killing the prison chaplain. Luckily for that chaplain the raid didn't come to fruition.

Charles did not seem too disheartened; sustained by strong ale, he entertained the local populace by gesticulating with a chicken leg and boasting of each son's prowess as a horse thief as they came out to be hanged.

I found it impossible to leave Aylesbury without dropping into the Kings Head. This fifteenth-century inn is one of the finest in the country. The building acted as a guesthouse for the Greyfriars monastery. Cromwell used it and it is alleged that his chair and bed are still *in situ*. There is a peg in the bedroom wall that permits one to listen to the conversation in the bar. There is also a spy window in the passage and a priest hole, which has a hidden entrance behind the lounge bar fireplace.

Aylesbury has the dubious honour of hanging the first murderer arrested because of the electric telegraph. In 1784 John Tawell was born in Aledby, a small village in Norfolk. At fourteen he took up a sort of apprenticeship with a widow at Lowestoft. The widow was a Quaker and Tawell found it convenient to follow that Christian denomination. The widow assembled herbal remedies and John delivered them all over East Anglia – he was a good salesman. He was also a charmer, a socialite, a womaniser and a comprehensive liar. However, outwardly he was respectable to the point of being engaged to a Quaker girl at Norwich. At the age of twenty, Tawell was befriended by Walter Hunton, a wealthy linen draper from London. Hunton was later hanged for highway robbery but prior to this he welcomed Tawell into the firm. Unfortunately, the same year John impregnated an Ipswich barmaid who insisted upon marriage; John complied.

Out of a job after the death of Hunton, Tawell took to the road selling goods. His life became opulent and colourful. He was honest in trade and popular with his colleagues. The only drawback to this lifestyle was a rather dull wife with an increasingly expensive brood of children. John fell foul of the law in 1814 when he forged a bank bond of £2,000 – a capital offence. The bank manager, also a Quaker, was loath to press charges that would result in Tawell being hanged. The police insisted. As a compromise Tawell was charged with possessing, rather than forging, the bond. Found guilty, he was transported to Australia indefinitely.

In Sydney, John Tawell's knowledge of medicines and amiable ways ingratiated him with the prison doctor. Four years later he was released. He then borrowed enough money to set up a drugstore in Sydney and two years later he had half a dozen similar establishments. After five years, business had trebled again – a meteoric rise in wealth and opulence.

The Kings Head, Aylesbury.

Unfortunately for Tawell, news of his success had travelled to England, where his dowdy wife had raised sufficient funds to come out looking for him. On her arrival, Mrs Tawell was infuriated to the extreme to find that John had not only amassed a fortune but had also collected a vast following of female devotees. As at least two of these devotees, who were anticipating becoming 'Mrs Tawell', now discovered, there already was a Mrs Tawell. John decided that it might be a suitable time to return to England and live the rest of his life in rich comfort.

In England Tawell started a profitable export company, sailing to Australia on a regular basis. The loss of one of his sons had a lasting effect upon him; it certainly did on his wife, who became a very sick woman. Ever attentive, Tawell engaged a live-in nurse, Sarah Hart. Soon Sarah was spending as much time in Tawell's bed as she was at his wife's bedside. Inevitably Sarah became pregnant and conveniently Mrs Tawell died. The next couple of years were blissfully happy for the pair, Sarah being rewarded with another child.

The cottage at Bath Place, Salt Hill.

In 1838 Tawell became infatuated with Mrs Cutforth, another Quaker and headmistress of the girls' school. Tawell proposed, but this time the Quakers objected. Mrs Cutforth was the widow of a member of the hierarchy. Defying the elder Quakers, Mrs Cutforth became the second Mrs Tawell and moved into a house at Berkhampsted, along with the widow's daughter.

Sarah Hart, now a nagging inconvenience, was settled into a cottage at Salt Hill, Slough. The new Mrs Tawell was fully aware of Sarah and her offspring. It is therefore strange that Tawell took such drastic action is to rid himself of an inconvenience.

John collected two phials of prussic acid from Bishopsgate. Arriving at 4 p.m. on 1 January at Salt Hill, John suggested to Sarah that they have a drink at the nearby Windmill Inn. Much now is supposition, but we know that the pair returned to the cottage. Shortly afterwards, John is witnessed swiftly leaving the scene and Sarah is found screaming then moaning in the cottage. A neighbour, Mary Ashley, called for a Dr Champney, but he arrived too late to save Sarah Hart's life. Hearing Mary Ashley's description of 'a Quaker' (Mary did not know Tawell), Champney decided to give chase.

Tawell reached Slough station where he caught a coach west to Windsor. At Windsor he returned to Slough and caught the 7.45 train to London. Tawell had two pieces of bad luck. One was the coach driver who noticed his strange behaviour at Windsor station; the other was the tenacious Champney who was watching Slough station. The resourceful doctor watched Tawell mount the train and then instructed railway staff to telegraph police at Bishops Road terminus. A Sergeant Williams followed Tawell around several London coffee houses before watching him enter his night's lodging at Cheapside. The police raided the lodgings at 7 a.m. but the bird had already flown. He was later arrested at the Jerusalem Coffee House where he swore he'd never heard of Sarah Hart or Salt Hill. Tawell was taken to Eton police station where he was charged with the murder of Sarah Hart before being escorted to Aylesbury to await trial.

The official trial began at Aylesbury on 12 March 1845, before Judge Baron Parke. The prosecution called thirty witnesses on the first day, the most condemning testimony coming from Dr Champney. The most melodramatic evidence came from Sarah Hart's mother, who theatrically fainted whilst giving evidence.

It was hardly surprising that Tawell's contrived alibi wasn't believed; he stated at the trial that he had been present when a hysterical and drunken Sarah Hart had committed suicide in front of him. He panicked and fled. Once again he was not believed. Nor was Tawell's counsel believed when he insulted the jury's intelligence by suggesting that Sarah had died from prussic acid poisoning through eating too many apples. The trial ended on the third day. Judge Baron Parke took four hours summing up but the jury took far less time to bring a guilty verdict.

Tawell was physically shaken – he had been confident enough of acquittal to order a celebration dinner at the White Hart Hotel. John Tawell admitted his guilt in Aylesbury Prison before meeting his maker in the Market Square on the 28 March 1845.

Piddington is a leafy border village just across in Oxfordshire. It is set in a hollow and has many winding and lonely lanes. It was just off of one of these lanes that the body of a gentleman, Johnny Edmonds, aged thirty-five was discovered at 10 a.m. one April morning in early 1880. The body was in a mess; the head had almost been decapitated.

The gruesome sight was discovered by a travelling draper named Thomas Plenderleith from Berkhampsted. He went for help and returned with the police, forewarning them about the state of the body and suggesting that it had been hit by a horse and cart.

Johnny had started his working life as a farm labourer. However, he was not well suited to the hard physical work and it was not long before he had learned the basics of clock and watch repairing. He then travelled Oxfordshire and the surrounding counties mending timepieces and making quite a prosperous living.

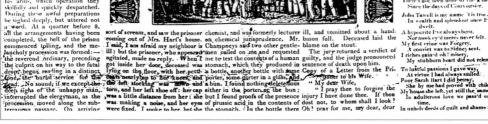

A newspaper article report on the execution of John Tawell at Aylesbury.

Inspector George Webb did not agree with Plenderleith's diagnosis that it had been a road accident. Webb knew it to be murder and he also knew Gentleman Johnny always carried cash and valuable small items with him. Webb's priority was to discover where the travelling watch mender had spent the evening previous to his demise.

The inspector's search did not take long. The landlord of the Seven Stars at Ludgershall, just about 3 miles from Piddington, knew Johnny fairly well and remembered that he had visited the premises the previous evening and stayed until late, a fact that was borne out by several other regular customers. They also recalled that the clock mender and pedlar was showing some very expensive trinkets. The landlord was also able to supply Inspector Webb with the name and address of no less than four labourers that Johnny had been socialising with.

Inspector Webb called first on William Dumbleton at a small cottage he shared with his mother, brother and two sisters. Dumbleton was outraged at the suggestion that he had been involved in a murder. He denied any involvement venomously and repeatedly. However, his attitude changed somewhat when one of Webb's officers entered with a very expensive watch, known to have belonged to Johnny – he realised that it could only have been discovered on his premises.

A second story soon emerged: Dumbleton had followed John Edmonds with his friend James Sharpe. They had got ahead of their intended victim by taking short cuts and waited behind a hedge. Gesturing to Dumbleton to stay behind a hedge, Sharpe borrowed his knife, walked across to Edmonds, knocked him to the ground, slit his throat, robbed him and chucked him in the ditch.

Later Dumbleton made a statement admitting that he had been with Sharpe all of the time and later still he admitted that he'd been the one to cut Edmonds' throat. The trial of William Dumbleton opened on 20 April 1880 at Northampton Assizes. James Sharpe was strongly suspected of being involved locally but there was not significant evidence to arrest him, let alone charge him. It did not take the jury long to find William Dumbleton guilty. He went quietly to the gallows on Monday 10 May 1880. His execution was the final one to be held at Aylesbury.

BISHOPSTONE

Bishopstone lies roughly midway between Stone and Aston Clinton. It was here that there lived a witch who could ride hurdles. She would straddle a hurdle, whisper the magic words and the wooden structure would take off at an incredible rate, rising several feet in the air. Well, if you believe a broomstick why not a hurdle?

Bishopstone's flying witch straddles her hurdle. *(Brenda Allaway)*

BOARSTALL

I am greatly indebted to Jennifer Westwood and Jacqueline Simpson for much of the information here and in several other stories. Their book, *The Lore of the Land*, is one of my most prized possessions.

The rather creepy Boarstall Tower is all that remains of the great house; the remainder of the building was demolished by Sir John Aubrey in 1738. The story of the demolition of the great house is a tragic tale indeed. When Sir John's son was about five years old, he refused his gruel. His nurse, thinking she would liven it up with some sugar, inadvertently used some oatmeal and arsenic that was used for the disposal of rodents. The boy died, and his mother, who never got over it, died within the year. Sir John could no longer stand the place and had it demolished.

A copy of an 1830s view of Boarstall, a fortified manor house. *(Brenda Allaway)*

Boarstall is said to get its name from one Nigel Shortshirt. It was once in the centre of Bernwood Forest a favourite hunting ground of Edward the Confessor. The trouble was that the area was infested with wild boar. Nigel endeared himself to the king by presenting him with the head of a massive boar. In appreciation, the grateful king presented Nigel Shortshirt with the arable land of Derehyde, a wood called Hulewode, Bernwood Forest and a horn, which was symbolic of his entitlement of the land for his heirs of the future. It must be stated that there is very little to substantiate the story and that grateful monarchs bestowing gifts for the riddance of boars is a very common theme in folklore.

BUCKLAND

Worn and hardly recognisable in Buckland is an effigy of the last man hanged at Hangman's Hill. The unlikely resting place of this figure is above the priest's door of the parish church.

A headless horseman is reputed to ride the Icknield Way at Butlers Cross. This unlikely spirit haunts the stretch of Iron Age roadway between Chequer and Wellwick Farm.

CHEARSLEY

I am indebted to Hilary Stainer Rice for the following haunted Chearsley stories. Hilary in turn claims to be indebted to two local historians.

Apparently the poltergeist activity at Farthing Cottage has been attributed to a presence nicknamed 'Old George'. There seems to be no corroborative evidence as to whether or not 'Old George' was ever in residence at the cottage. However, his spirit was in evidence for nearly twenty-five years after the Second World War. The poltergeist activity seems to have been mild rather than ferocious; 'Old George' moved articles around rather than propelled them.

As far as the record goes, George was only seen on one occasion. The next-door neighbour's godson entered the premises inadvertently. He came across the shade of an old man in a white suit. His hair was also snowy white and he was counting money at a table.

Could the cottage once have belonged to a miserly Old George? Could the poltergeist activity be caused by the spirit of the old man, returning and looking for a hidden cache? Fanciful I admit, but were I the owner of Farthing Cottage I would think it worth a look around.

Chearsley's jovial rat catcher. (*Brenda Allaway*)

There is another very sad little story about a tragedy that happened in 1915, when a young girl died in a fire. Many years later a resident in the same cottage had nightmares about being burned.

Lastly, there is also a story about a local rat catcher. It was this gentleman's wont to stuff live mice under his top hat. He would arrange his time schedule so that he was passing the village school at going home time. Approaching a group of schoolgirls he would politely raise his hat, thoroughly enjoying the screams as the small rodents ran amok.

CHOLESBURY

Cholesbury church is built inside the remains of a hill fort. This is unusual but by no means unique. It is thought that a type of exorcism was the Christian intention in building churches on much honoured pagan sites. Personally I've always found some of the ancient pagan sites in the Cholesbury area a little disconcerting.

DINTON

Part of the attraction of follies is that they decay with such dignity. However, Dinton Castle, Sir John van Hatten's 1769 construction, seems to have passed the point of no return. The floors have rotted away and the once attractive tower heads have gone. Stuart Barton in the book *Monumental Follies* states that 'A latticework of ivy provides a living overcoat, holding the crumbling walls together'.

The castle was originally built to house John van Hatten's vast collection of fossils, many of which were incorporated in the structure of its walls. Later the building was used as accommodation for the servants of the manor house. One hopes it was a little less draughty than today.

Do not leave Dinton without having a look at the church and its Saxon carvings. Also for those with the inclination there is whipping post and stocks for inspection.

The village of Ford, some 2 miles away, has a pub which commemorates the Dinton hermit, John Bigg. Bigg was born in 1596. He became secretary to Simon Mayne, a landowner from the same village. Mayne was a friend of Cromwell and one of the panel of judges that sentenced Charles I to death. It is thought that John Bigg was the masked man that actually decapitated the king. Naturally, after the restoration, Mayne was not popular and was imprisoned. Bigg, though not officially charged with anything, had what can only be described as a mental

Clockwise from above:

Dinton Folly.

The Dinton Hermit Inn.

The stocks at Dinton church.

breakdown. He gave away his not inconsiderable wealth and dwelt in a cave, living on charity. Disillusioned as he was, Bigg still had a sense of priorities. It is said that he always carried three flasks in his girdle: one of strong beer, one of small beer and one of milk.

EDLESBOROUGH

Edlesborough seems a natural home for ghosts. Reputedly there are at least four in the village. Church Farm is believed to have one called 'Jack the Leather' or 'Old Leather Breeches'. Apparently, Jack was a highwayman who was in hiding at the farm. Lacking exercise, he mounted the horses and went for a ride around the farm at night. Unfortunately for Jack a keen-eyed villager noticed that the horses were lathered in the morning, he called the troopers out and Jack was dragged from hiding. His ghost still re-enacts his final night's ride.

The publication by the Women's Institute informs me of a ghost at the old vicarage. It is said to be the spirit of the gardener who was murdered in a brawl between two feuding families.

Charity Farm has a greatly disturbed ghost. The spirit is said to be that of a farm worker who hanged himself in a threshing room. The farm is now a private development and the floor level has changed; this could be the reason why, when the spectre appears, only half of him is visible.

I'm afraid to say that we have another Dick Turpin here. Poor old Dick, whatever he did in life, no poor ghost should be expected to haunt over 300 sites. This time our overworked Dick watches from a manor house at Northall. He is said to be studying the coaches labouring their way up the Ivinghoe Beacon, thus giving himself time to ride out and rob them as they entered Dunstable.

ELLESBOROUGH

As one might expect from its ancient appearance, the parish church at Ellesborough sports a ghost or two. Firstly, there is the 'tall man dressed in mediaeval garb', as the surprised organist described him, who was one of many to witness the phantom over the years. A flower-arranger noted the spectre one afternoon and a visitor from far afield was also disturbed by the apparition.

One often wonders with ghostly apparitions if there is a certain amount of psychological suggestion. If a place is known to be haunted then an individual in possession of that prior knowledge is more disposed to experience something strange. Often it is almost a chicken and egg situation, did the story manufacture

The haunted church at Ellesborough.

Haunted pews at Ellesborough church.

the ghost? Or, did the ghost bring about the relating of the story? Does psychic phenomena, like gossip, feed upon itself? In many cases I suspect it does. It is therefore refreshing to find apparitions such as Ellesborough's mediaeval man witnessed by uninitiated strangers.

This particular ghost is reported to glide over towards the memorial tablets and disappear within. One courageous visitor had the presence of mind to follow the spirit to its destination – this would seem to be the Hawtry Memorial plaque. I'm afraid I know little of the Hawtrys, aside from giving the nearby Chequers its present form. The portrait brass here shows Sir Thomas Hawtry dressed in armour, with his wife, eleven sons and eight daughters. One is permitted the flippant thought that the spectral figure might be one of the family who was left behind in some family exodus. The second spectre is yet another lady in white. She is reputed to be the unrequited love of Revd Robert Wallis who spent a brief two-year period at Ellesborough before resigning.

On a recent visit to Ellesborough's church a local lady showed me a pew that she claimed was used by two spectral female worshippers.

I am once again indebted to Hilary Stainer Rice for informing me of a second haunted building at Ellesborough. It concerns a sixteenth-century barn that has been converted into a house. The spectre here takes the form of a smock-attired farmhand. This very well attested ghost seems cheerful and benign. He has been witnessed setting about his daily chores with a cheerful attitude. We are told that there have been no tragic deaths at the building, as far as local historians can ascertain. Then indeed why should there be; if there is any logic whatsoever in the spirit world is it not more likely that spirits, whatever they are, should return to a place at which they have been content?

EYTHROPE

Westwood and Simpson's *The Lore of the Land* informs us of Horace Harman gathering stories for his *Sketches of the Bucks Countryside* in 1934. Harman was informed by an ancient yokel that a little witch was often seen by him sitting on a hurdle. One could always tell when he/she was about because the sheep had been transfixed by the figure and were staring in the witch's general direction. The witch had a figure like a balloon, long legs and a pickid (pockmarked) nose. As the teller of the tale got nearer the little person jumped on the hurdle and galloped away.

Another ancient countryman informed Harman that he had been a night-watchman at Eythrope House (sadly long gone). On his rounds with his dog one night he approached the pavilion and saw what looked like a group of rabbits. His dog became excited. As he neared the site he became aware that the 'rabbits' were little men. They had extremely funny faces and danced and frolicked at will. They were aware, but took no notice, of the watchman or his dog.

The countryman stated that the little men were once a regular sight but had not been seen for some years. He went on to inform Harman that there were ghosts at the old house and many strange goings-on that he thought were instigated by Lord Stanhope. Personally, I can find little information on this gentleman. Whether he indulged in the occult is open to speculation.

GRANBOROUGH

I am indebted to *The Buckinghamshire Village Book* for a brief note on Granborough Lodge, once the local vicarage. It is reputed to be haunted by a village vicar who was unfortunately drowned at Scarborough. Quite an ambitious trip even if taken in spirit, one might think.

GREAT KIMBLE

The village is reputedly named after Cunobelinus, a part-legendary British king, who, mythology dictates, died in AD 43. Shakespeare's *Cymbeline* was based on this character. Cymbeline's Castle is also the name of the Celtic earthwork in nearby Chequers Park, which has given rise to the superstition that if one runs around the mound seven times the devil will appear. There could be some truth in this outlandish story because Prime Ministers are witnessed in profusion.

GRENDON

The Ship Inn in the village is sadly no longer. It was there that Shakespeare visited on his trips from London to Stratford. It is also rumoured that the Bard penned *A Midsummer Nights Dream* and *Much Ado about Nothing* at the old Ship. Apparently he modelled his characters on some of the locals.

HADDENHAM

A strangely decorated folly stands in the centre of Haddenham. It is the Bone House in the High Street. Apparently in 1807, when the cottage was constructed, the poorer person built with whatever came to hand and one of the most plentiful commodities in this neck of the woods was dead sheep. An imaginative builder incorporated knucklebones into the walls to form animal faces, hearts, diamonds and tools. Pride of place went to the date '1807' on this most unique of buildings.

Years ago Haddenham gained the prefix of 'Silly' due to the legend of silly Haddenham: in those days the village was famous for its ducks and one man who was justifiably proud of his feathered friends constructed a roof over his pond to keep them dry during inclement weather.

In 1828 a gardener from Haddenham saw two men, Sewell and Tyler, steal a sheep. The gardener, Noble Edden, did not report the theft, knowing that sheep stealing meant a sentence of death or at the very least transportation. Edden, being a man with a sense of humour, could not resist the temptation to bleat like a sheep every time he came across the thieves in town. His humour cost him dearly, for his mimicking alarmed Sewell and Tyler to such an extent that they decided to stop his bleating for good.

The same evening Mrs Edden had an apparition of her husband being waylaid by two men and his skull being fractured by a stone. In her vision she saw Tyler dealing the fatal blow. When her husband failed to return Mrs Edden raised the alarm. A search party was set up and the gardener's body was soon discovered.

Haddenham's Bone House.

It was almost a year before the pair were arrested. Sewell confessed to the crime and he and Tyler took the drop at Aylesbury Prison in 1830.

Edden's ghost has been witnessed on several occasions in a lane at Haddenham that branches off the A418. Be careful – it brings bad luck to whoever meets it.

ICKNIELD WAY

This is a prehistoric track that runs across England from the Wash to Wiltshire. At various stages through Buckinghamshire and Oxford it is reputedly haunted by Roman legionnaires, Black dogs and Boadicea in her chariot.

IVINGHOE

Ivinghoe is where the Icknield Way forks, where the ancient windmill can be seen picturesque against the sky and where Beacon Hill rises 760ft skyward. There is a hoary church tower and an inn with an Elizabethan stone fireplace.

What isn't so generally known is that Ivinghoe suggested to Sir Walter Scott the name of his hero Ivanhoe, in the book of that name.

There is a jingle in the village as old as the Chiltern Hills. There are many versions, the best known states:

> Tring, Wing and Ivinghoe
> Hampden of Hampden did forgo
> For striking of Ye Prince a blow
> And glad he might escapen so.

Hampden (1594-1643) is the Parliamentarian John Hampden, who is reputed to have lost his lands after striking the Black Prince. Did the luckless Hampden clove the prince's head with a sword? No, legend states that he hit him around the ear with a tennis racket after disputing a point.

KINGWOOD

Kingwood is reputed to be one of the secret places that Henry II hid his mistress Fair Rosamund. The rather tenuous evidence seems to be based on the village's name and ancient lane known as Rosiman's Waye.

Sir Walter Scott was so impressed with Ivinghoe that he called his famous novel, *Ivanhoe*, after a slightly altered name of the village.

Ivinghoe village was a costly loss of temper for John Hampden.

THE LEES

The remains of British and Roman settlements abound here. Slightly less ancient is the Cock and Rabbit Inn. The original hostelry was built in the 1750s but it was demolished by the lord of the manor who found that the ribald songs and noisy joviality of drunken villagers was not conducive with his justified repose.

It is not known when the present building was erected or how the unique name was acquired. A rather mundane explanation is that the original landlord promoted cock fighting and bred rabbits. There is also a rather vague account of a spectral haywain passing the door.

Old Inn House on Lee Common is, as its name suggests, a private dwelling. The ghost seems to remain in the street, the orchard and the tennis court. Hilary Stainer Rice describes the Phantom Lady as 'an ethereal grey/white shimmering figure'. It would seem that the owner and his wife had both witnessed the shade on separate occasions but for some time didn't mention it to each other for fear of ridicule.

One could not leave this area without mentioning the renowned massive figurehead. It is obviously a ship's head and is a naval-looking gentleman in officer's uniform. I have recently discovered this gentleman is Admiral Earl Howe. The figurehead was retrieved when the last wooden warship was broken up and the planks used in the construction of the Liberty Store in Regent Street.

Uncanny happenings were often reported at the Cock and Rabbit, a pub at The Lees.

The impressive figurehead of Admiral Howe at The Lees.

Littleworth Common had sightings of a puma. *(Brenda Allaway)*

LITTLEWORTH COMMON

Littleworth Common has a quite authenticated sighting of a wild puma. It was seen in the area in November 1964. The animal was witnessed some thirty times in a massive area stretching from Northamptonshire to the Sussex coast.

LONG CRENDON

It was thought to be the ancient lace-makers of this majestic village that inspired Shakespeare in *Twelfth Night* to make his clown sing:

> The spinsters and knitters in the sun
> And the free maids that weave their thread with bones
> Do use to chant it.

Long Crendon has strong associations with William Shakespeare.

Henry IV gave a great house at Long Crendon to Catherine after Agincourt. He told the lovely Catherine the house was hers if she would say 'Harry of England I am thine.' Other gifts he promised his beloved were, I quote, 'England is thine, Ireland is thine, France is thine and Henry Plantagenet is thine.' Catherine's Court House is a proud possession of the village and is reputed to be one of the earliest acquisitions of the National Trust.

83

Shakespeare wrote *Twelfth Night* and *A Midsummer Nights Dream* at Crendon Underwood.

Once a year, in springtime, Long Crendon becomes a splash of colour. At one end of the street near the Eight Bells, the church and the aforementioned courthouse, floodlights abound from the church as locals put on a production of selections from the York Cycle of Mystery Plays. The display of colourful and liberally attired people lasts a week and apparently is a spectacle to behold.

Long Crendon also has a host of ghosts, most of which I was informed about went I last visited the village in 2005. I was informed that they were all benign. Benign possibly, but not all cheerful.

The courthouse has experienced quite an appreciable amount of poltergeist activity over the centuries. However, there seems to have been little notable action for about a decade.

We have a horseman, or possibly a horsewoman, at Lower End. The rider has been described as grey in colour and the galloping hooves make no sound. There is another figure in grey, this time definitely female, who abides in or near the church. She is shy or coy, but she is said to smile as she disappears.

The saddest ghost and probably the most intriguing is a little lady who seems to be rather upset. The legend is that she is searching for her soul. One would think that she had little chance of retrieving it. For some fathomless reason it was apparently taken from the little lady, placed in a salt box and buried in a chimney wall at the Mound. I wish I could discover more of the final story but I deem it unlikely that I will.

LONG MARSTON

Long Marston is generally lumped together with Puttenham and the hamlets of Astrope and Gubblecote. For a long time it was a Mecca for the followers of witchcraft. Pilgrimages were made here to view the pond (some say stream) where Ruth Osborne, England's last witch, was murdered. Sad to say the stream/pond has now dried up and seekers of witchcraft and the occult no longer visit the village and Long Marston's one claim to fame no longer exists. But let us delve a little deeper into Ruth Osborne.

Officially the last execution of a witch was in 1682 and the last conviction for witchcraft was 'proved' against Jane Wenham in 1712. Jane was found guilty at Hereford Assizes but the judge obtained a pardon, much to the chagrin of numerous farmers who claimed she had bewitched their labourers. Fast forward now to the Tring area of Hertfordshire where in 1751 an old couple were accused of witchcraft and 'executed' by a mob.

John and Ruth lived in Long Marston. They were very old, in their seventies, and also very poor. In 1745 they had been supporters of the Stuart rebellion, which had not endeared them to some of their neighbours. It was strongly rumoured that the pair indulged in witchcraft. The suspicion was endorsed when mother Osborne approached John Butterfield, a local farmer, and asked him for some buttermilk. The farmer refused and on returning home found some of his cows dying. It was obvious to him that Ruth Osborne had put a curse upon him. Terrified now of farming, Butterfield sold up and took a pub, the Black Horse, at Gubblecote. Unfortunately for Butterfield bad luck followed him there. He developed some boils and sores and also became prone to fits. After referring to a white witch at Northampton he was told, and deeply believed, that he been cursed by Ruth Osborne.

Rumour spread like wildfire, so much so that William Dell the town crier of Hemel Hempstead announced that a local couple suspected of witchcraft were to be ducked at Long Marston; similar announcements were made at Leighton Buzzard and Winslow.

Long Marston, home of suspected witch, Ruth Osborne. Ruth and her husband were murdered by a screaming mob

Terrified of mob rule, officials secreted the couple in a local workhouse. The mob, ably led by Thomas Colley, a chimney sweep, descended on the workhouse where they smashed windows, broke down pales and searched everywhere. Even the salt box that could not hold anything larger than the average cat was scrutinised. Everybody knew that a witch like Ruth Osborne would have no problem transmuting into a feline. Finally, when Colley threatened to burn down the building, the officials forced the Osbornes from their place of refuge. They were stripped naked, their thumbs were bound to their toes and they were dragged to Wilstone Weir to be ducked.

Ruth Osborne, tied in a sheet for modesty's sake, would not sink. Colley grabbed a staff, beat her and then held her underwater with it until she almost expired. She was then pulled out and whilst choking in the mud was beaten to death. John Osborne, who had received similar treatment, died a short time later.

Colley, proud of his actions, thought it appropriate to take a collection for himself. He was, however, less proud when he was charged with murder at Hertford Assizes on 30 July 1751. After being found guilty he was sentenced to be hanged in chains at Wilstone Weir. However, people living nearby protested and Colley met his maker on a gibbet at Gubblecote Cross. Colley's body rotted in chains there for some time. It gave rise to several ghost stories. The Revd Frederick Lee, writing in 1878, informs us that the parish clerk of Long Marston, accompanied by a lady and gentleman of that village, came across a spectral animal near a field named Gibraltar. For some unknown reason it was taken to be the spirit of Thomas Colley.

Even later, in 1911, the village schoolmaster came across Colley's canine ghost. This time the observer was being driven home in a gig when he noticed a small fire beside the road next to where the stunted remnants of Colley's gibbet stood. They pulled up with a jolt and sat staring in fear and silence at a massive black dog, 'gaunt and shaggy, with long ears and tail, eyes like balls of fire and large long teeth, for he seemed to grin at us.' The dog finally disappeared or 'to sink into the earth, and we drove over the spot where he had lain.' Ghosts returning a in the form of dogs was widely believed in the eighteenth century. Personally I can find no logic in the assumption whatsoever.

LONGWICK

Longwick is famous for its May Day garlands. Local children weave garlands from wild flowers and take them from house to house.

MENTMORE

Hilary Stainer Rice has a couple of tales from the village in her *Ghosts of the Chilterns and Thames Valley*. One concerns a lady of the village who in 1907 witnessed an old gentleman waving to her. Nothing strange about that, but the poor old chap had died the day before. The same lady also had visits from various relations who had died abroad in the wars.

Another tale from Mentmore, which Hilary mentions very briefly, is the story of the local vicar, John Horneby. Legend dictates that in 1697 Horneby saw a corpse approaching him. This so shocked him that he returned home and promptly hanged himself.

NORTH MARSTON

There is quite a nice little relic here in the shape of Sir John Shorne's Well or the Town Well. There is a spring here with healing powers. The water specialises in scorbutic and cutaneous diseases (ague and gout). It also cures a cold overnight. Shorne was rector here from 1290 to 1314 and graciously gave the well to the village. Hence the small verse:

> Sir John Shorne. Gentleman born.
> Conjured the devil into a horn.

For some unknown reason the final word horn was once boot. Another similar verse discovered later, but probably, judging from the English, composed far earlier runs:

> To maister John Shorne
> That blessed man borne
> For the ague to hym we apply
> Which jugeleth with a bote (boot)

One of Henry VIII's agents visiting North Marston in 1548 discovered a picture of Sir John squeezing a small devil into a boot. There is a strong school of thought that believes Sir John invented the original Jack in the Box.

The Devil in a Boot at North Marston. *(Brenda Allaway)*

QUAINTON

Quainton Hill, 613ft, is reputed to be the home of a whole host of goblins and fairies. From the same hill a group of horses, complete with headless riders, emerge.

In the village the old Rectory was given a cutting from the sacred Glastonbury thorn and, on a tract behind the building, a ghostly horseman canters. Whether he is headless and a renegade of those on the hill is unknown. Carters Lane, sometimes known as Gypsy Lane, is part of an old Roman road. There is an ancient stone dated 1641, which claims to be the headstone of the gypsy king. I have written literally hundreds of pages on gypsies and believe me there is at least one gypsy king in every county.

Quainton has another association with Romanies when, in living memory, a gypsy queen was buried at the local church. Apparently her vardlo (caravan) was burned outside. The burning of caravans and other goods was always extremely rare. As the Bard would say, 'It is a custom more honoured in the breach than the observance.'

Well-named Quainton is full of curious phenomena.

There are several monuments in Quainton church to the Dormer family. The earliest is to Fleetwood Dormer. There are others dedicated to his son, Sir John Dormer and his wife, and one to Sir Robert Dormer, a gifted lawyer whose son died at the age of thirty. His heartbroken father soon followed him to the grave.

In 1847 George Lipscomb describes how there was a black marble slab in the floor beneath which was the body of Susanna, Lady Dormer, wife of Sir John Dormer.

The story goes that Sir John Dormer, residing in Italy after the death of his wife, was continually upset by dreams of her floating in water. So disturbed was Sir John that he returned and had his beloved resurrected. The coffin was exactly as he had dreamed, surrounded by water. Some stories relate that the body was perfectly intact. There has been some credence given to this unlikely story based generally on theories concerning the absorption of water.

RIDGEWAY PATH

The Ridgeway is thought to have been a trading route but its origins are clouded in the mists of time. It is roughly 85 miles in length and stretches from Silbury Hill near Avebury in the south-western end to Ivinghoe Beacon at the north-eastern end.

The main mysteries, apart from Avebury, are the 'castles' or hill forts. It is still a matter of debate whether these massive round earthworks at Liddington, Barbury, Uffington and Segsbury were Iron Age settlements or staging posts along a trade route.

ST LEONARDS

Hilary Stainer Rice informs us of a haunting at Dundridge Manor at St Leonards. This fifteenth-century building has had associations with many famous names over the centuries. One of these was Margaret Pole who outlived her husband, Richard, Earl of Salisbury, but had to forfeit the property to the king, who promptly sold it on to Sir John Baldwin in 1544. Henry VIII later had Margaret thrown into the Tower of London. It has been suggested that the resident ghost, nicknamed Silkie because of her rustling clothing, might be the tragic Margaret, who stayed at the manor *en route* to the Tower. Another strong candidate for Silkie is that she was a disturbed wife of one of the Baldwins. Whoever she is, Silkie's appearances are somewhat limited; her footsteps in a corridor are restricted to warm afternoons from August to October.

Another audible ghost is heard in the winter. There is not much to report other than the supernatural knocking on the door at the bottom of the stairs. There is a report that two young boys were fighting there some 120 years ago and one slew the other with a ploughshare. The rattling and knocking on the door is thought to be the fatally wounded boy trying to escape the aggressor.

SLAPTON

Once again I am indebted to *The Buckinghamshire Village Book* for the information recorded in the *Northampton Mercury* regarding the trial of a witch on 2 July 1770. The unfortunate woman was to be tried by the water ordeal, otherwise known as floating, and then weighed against a Bible. But the miller who was detailed to perform the 'trial' at Slapton Mill, refused because there were too many people about. However, he promised to perform the 'trial' later. Whether or not he kept his promise is not recorded.

Slapton's ghosts are recorded in the *Village Book*, but I had come across them on previous ghost hunts in Buckinghamshire. The first is a benign old lady clad in black who wanders along a disused and overgrown footpath carrying a basket.

The second is one of the strangest I have heard of in the fifty years I have spent studying the subject. It is the buckles of a pair of shoes belonging to a one-time rector of the village: it is assumed that the invisible reverend gentleman's ghost is still wearing them, as they seemed to move at a hurrying pace.

The third involves two ghosts; a young girl runs hither and thither, apparently searching for her phantom horse that can be seen running in the opposite direction.

Finally there is an old cottage where the ghostly cries of children can be heard.

STONE

There is an inexplicable carving on the Norman font of St John the Baptist's Church at Stone. It is perhaps one of the great iconographic enigmas of the mediaeval world. Included in the panel are two naked men, aided by a very large bird, attacking a monster. A snake lies beneath the foot of one of the men. The man's leg is being attacked by a lizard or salamander. Whilst sitting on his haunches, seemingly watching the whole affair, is a fire-breathing dragon. At the dragon's back is a vertical fish. The whole meaning and any explanation of the mysterious panel has been lost in the mists of time.

A couple had to be re-housed by the local authority at Stone because their previous council house was haunted by an earlier tenant, an old lady who had died of heart attack. The young couple, who had only seen the old girl once, refused point blank to step over the threshold again. I have withheld the names and addresses for the sake of privacy.

Another story accredited to Horace Harman and brought to life by Westwood and Simpson is the Witch of Stone. A carter was encouraging his team of four up Eythrope Hill. Arriving at the top the horses, complete with load of wheat, would go no further. The horses shivered and shook but could not be encouraged to move. It was then the carter noticed an old woman standing against her front gate peering at them. The man, being of country stock, realised immediately what was amiss and remedied the situation; walking up to the old hag, he struck her hard across the hand, causing blood to flow. The horses were soon on their way, contentedly. The carter explained that, 'When the blood flows the spell's broke.'

UPHILL

Near to St Leonards is Uphill, close to an enclosed reservoir and an old Iron Age hill fort. On cloudy and moonless nights in the forest here, strange animal noises are heard. They are generally experienced near to a place where a gibbet once stood, aptly named Hang Hill. The noises are described as gnawing, screeching, biting and burrowing noises. The rare glimpses of these animals suggest they are black pigs or boars. The spectral animals have been witnessed battering each other, but there are never any traces of the disturbance on the ground the following morning.

Several explanations have been put forward to explain the phenomenon. The grisliest is that there was an attack on the Iron Age fort. It was rebuffed and many of the attackers were slain. They were the lucky ones. Legend dictates that the wounded were distributed to the wild boars that populated the nearby hills. Pleasant little story, isn't it.

WENDOVER

Wendover is a Chiltern town with the Icknield Way as its thoroughfare. It is surrounded by Boddington Hill, Backham Hill and the magnificent 845ft Coombe Hill. On a clear day, from this splendid height, it is easy to discern St Paul's Cathedral 30 miles away, and from the same hill one can inspect an obelisk erected to the memory of Wendover men who fell in the Boer War.

The ancient Red Lion at Wendover was frequented by Cromwell and has experienced inexplicable supernatural phenomena.

John Hampden lived at Wendover in the manor house and his spectre is purported to remain at the Red Lion, an ancient inn that was also patronised by Robert Louis Stevenson.

Wendover became famous for hand lace-making accidentally. There is a holiday for all workers in the trade on the 25 November; it is known as St Catherine's day. Catherine was the lace-makers' patron saint but the Wendover celebrations are thought to be more in honour of Catherine of Aragon. Catherine became Henry VIII's first wife in 1509. Legend dictates that whilst staying near Wendover all her lace garments were accidentally burned. Catherine immediately ordered a new supply of lace clothing from the town. The fashionable court ladies were soon to follow the Queen's example and lace-making flourished in the town for several centuries.

The church at Wendover is situated half a mile outside the old town. Legend has it that it had been the intention to build it in the centre, but local witches were not pleased about the situation, and at night they carried the stones to the present site. The old site is still known as Witches Meadow.

WESTON TURVILLE

An epitaph in the churchyard reminds passers-by of a local double tragedy. Two brothers, James and Frederick Bates, were drowned in 1868 when they fell through the ice at Millpond. The epitaph reads:

> They sank beneath the frozen wave
> None to rescue none to save
> Tempted to death in sportive play
> These brothers sleep on Jesus day.

WHITCHURCH

Creslow Manor stands 6 miles north of Aylesbury. It is a very picturesque old house with quite a history. At one time it was outside the main parish and had a population of five. Creslow derives its name from 'Christ's Low' or 'Christ's Meadow' and was once the smallest parish in the county with the largest pasture (327 acres).

Cresslow Manor near Whitchurch.

The ancient ground was bought by the mysterious Knights Templars in 1120. There were many additions to the old building in Elizabethan days and also in the time of Charles I. Henry VIII claimed and confiscated the building and transformed it from a partly ecclesiastical building to secular ownership. The property later reverted to the Crown but was leased to Sir Thomas Clifford and later became the property of his successor, Lord Clifford, in 1673.

It is from this time that the ghostly manifestations began to appear. The rustling Lady is said to have been one of Clifford's wives. She is known as Rosamund. Around 1850 the sheriff of Buckingham treated the whole story with disdain and offered to sleep in the haunted chamber. He had a far from peaceful night. The sheriff could not be found in the morning and the door was locked and had to be broken open. When the gentleman returned he stated that he had experienced two encounters with an unseen lady, who was apparently attired in a long rustling dress. The sheriff had decided that it was expedient to spend the rest of the night somewhere else! Believers of the supernatural had received an unexpected convert.

Hilary Stainer Rice's *Ghosts of the Chilterns and Thames Valley* informs us about a spectral cat that haunted a cottage in the village. The phantom feline seems to have put in many appearances in the 1970s, upsetting its earthbound counterparts in the process.

WHITELEAF CROSS,

NR MONKS RISBOROUGH

There are over fifty figures engraved in our chalk hillsides. Most are fairly recent but Whiteleaf Cross is one of the few lost in the obscurities of time. Situated in the Chiltern Hills, facing the Vale of Aylesbury, it may be seen for some 15 miles. During the last couple of centuries the cross has actually grown by a few inches due to the excessive scouring. As with the White Horse at Uffington, scouring days were an excuse for a great celebration, attracting livestock sales and every conceivable sideshow.

The cross has always looked more like a sword being drawn from a stone to me, but I am no authority. Why it was ever placed there is open to much conjecture; was it a landmark for travellers walking in nearby Icknield Way? Was it a phallic symbol changed into a cross by the early monks of Missenden Abbey? Or was it cut by Christianised Saxons in celebration of beating off the Danes?

In 1855 a local clergyman was in no doubt of the intentions of the creators of the Whiteleaf Cross. On first seeing the hillside figure he felt inspired and impassioned enough to write the following colourful sentences:

Bursting for the first time on the eye of the traveller from the northern direction it presents an awful an almost spectral apparition of the sign of the Son of man looming heavenward above the peaceful valley, beside the ancient and everlasting hills.

WING

Ascott House, roughly a mile from Wing, has a very unusual feature: a topiary sundial. The dial has Roman figures cut from box hedges. A well-trimmed yew tree acts as the gnomon, pointing to the various times. Even more impressive are other box hedges cut to form the words 'Light and shade by turn, but always love.'

WINGRAVE

On the Sunday nearest to St Peter's Day children bring grass into the Church of St Peter and St Paul at Wingrave. I believe this is part of St Peter's patronage

Wingrave, home of St Peter's Day celebrations and witch Susanna Hannocks.

ceremony and the grass remains for a week. Another theory is that the ceremony came from the old practice of rush spreading (rushes were traditionally spread on the church floor to protect against the cold). At Wingrave the grass is supplied from a nearby field that was bequeathed to the church by a local lady. Legend states that one night she lost her way and nearly died from exposure, until finally finding the path home by following the sound of the church bells.

A slightly less pleasant little ceremony was once held at Wingrave. Susanna Hannocks, an old woman at the village, was accused of witchcraft. Her crime was bewitching a neighbour's spinning wheel and impairing its productivity. Her ordeal, although strange, was not unusual; Susanna was weighed against the Bible. Luckily she was heavier and therefore adjudged innocent.

3

NORTH BUCKINGHAMSHIRE

AKELEY

The Greyhound Inn at Akeley is reputedly haunted. In the 1950s the landlady heard footsteps in one of the bedrooms whilst she was below in the bar. The inn was closed at the time and all of the doors and windows were secured. Summoning her courage the lady searched upstairs, but found nobody.

More footsteps were heard by the landlady's daughter shortly after. Little was done to abate the weird wanderings; in fact the family became quite accustomed to this benign and friendly shade. The footsteps became a regular occurrence and a conversation subject over the following decade. Subsequent landlords, however, have experienced nothing unusual.

The Greyhound Inn (now a private house) at Akeley was reputedly haunted.

The Greyhound is an old coaching inn and also possesses a priest's hole. Perhaps the ancient inhabitant of this reclusive place was responsible for the phantom footsteps. The Greyhound is now a private residence, please respect.

Hilary Stainer Rice, in her book *Ghosts of the Chilterns and Thames Valley*, conducted another interview with the aforementioned landlady. This time, the lady recounted a spectral meeting she had experienced with a female figure in a white cowl at a local church.

BLETCHLEY

There is a story of Bletchley that concerns a phantom nurse or hospital worker. The story is told in Peter Moss's *Ghosts over Britain* by a reverend gentleman now living in Lincoln.

The reverend stated that in the 1950s he served as a medical orderly at RAF Benton. It was apparently an on-site sick quarters for minor injuries, not a place for the stress and intense emotions of the far more seriously afflicted.

A spiritual lady dressed in green became a quite well attested and acceptable phenomenon. She was diligent and regular in her duties. The writer himself claims to have heard, but never seen, this industrious spirit. Incidentally, green is not a colour generally favoured by ghosts.

BOW BRICKHILL

The village of Bow Brickhill makes its skyward ascension from the shimmering banks of the River Ouzel. Amongst the heath and pinewood here there is an ancient ditch and entrenchment, which, at one point, it is thought to be 55ft wide and nearly 20ft deep. The ditch's purpose is open to conjecture. It has been named Danes Borough, but it was constructed long before the Danes invaded.

The Buckinghamshire Village Book states that Dick Turpin rode the valleys here and that his phantom horse still drinks from a pond or stream here. This is, however, most unlikely.

Another colourful tale relates that an affluent lady bedecked by expensive jewels drove a coach and four into Blind Pond. The pond is believed to be so deep that it is said that the horses, coach and passenger are still in descent after a couple of centuries. The lady's ghost, that can occasionally be heard crying (not an easy thing to do when travelling downwards through water), seems to keep children away from the dangerous water.

Bow Brickhill, an unlikely venue for Dick Turpin, but there is something very strange at Blind Pond.

BUCKINGHAM

Buckingham is set in a loop of the River Ouse. When Alfred the Great divided his country into counties in AD 888, he named Buckingham as the county town. I am told that a swan welded on top of the clock at the Town Hall is there to remind us of past glory.

Unfortunately for Buckingham, in 1725 a fire destroyed most of the town centre, so the local government shifted to Aylesbury. Now, most of the town centre is an attractive mixture of Georgian architecture. There are, however, houses dating to far earlier periods that are definitely worth inspection. The thirteenth-century Chantry Chapel was rebuilt in 1475 as the Royal Latin School. It lies just off the market place and still has an attractive Norman doorway. The school was founded by Edward VI. Here, in a deep recess, is a doorway that was old when the Royalists fought with the Roundheads. One window here is adorned with grim looking heads. There is also a piscina (a stone basin containing holy water) and a gallery of six bench-ends with elaborate carvings from the seventeenth century.

The battlemented eighteenth-century castle sits in the centre of town. For many years it served as the county gaol. However, looking at its size one wonders if it

Buckingham's Old Gaol.

Buckingham's Castle House is said to be haunted, but which of its colourful tenants haunts it?

was adequate for the job. Did Buckinghamshire have very few convicted felons or were they packed in like sardines?

There must be hundreds of stories here; however, frustratingly, few or none were recorded. There would seem to be very few respectable ghosts in such an ancient town. Let us move on to Castle House.

It is difficult to ascertain which of the illustrious tenants of Castle House is responsible for haunting it. Rumour dictates that the most likely is Theophilus Adams who was the ecclesiastical confessor to Catherine of Aragon.

The building has been occupied by Buckingham Town Council since 1965 and at least since that time, a ghostly gentleman, thought to be Adams, has been seen in an upper corridor. There are, however, several other candidates for the spectre of Castle House. The occupants prior to the council have been as colourful as they have been controversial.

In the twelfth century Castle House was built from stones from an ancient castle destroyed by the Danes, later it became the seat of John Barton, a knight of the county. In 1431 John left it to his brother and shortly after it was taken over by the powerful Fowler family. It was Edward Fowler who entertained Catherine of Aragon. She gave birth to a son here, who unfortunately died within hours. Theophilus claimed the house had been used for 'superstitious purposes', John Barton having entertained some very strange people within.

In 1619 considerable alterations were made by the then owners, William and Mary Lambard. William died here soon after and is the second candidate for the spirit in the corridor.

Mary remarried, to Sir Edward Richardson whose friend Charles I was a regular visitor. Charles I indulged in a council of war here with the Prince of Wales and Prince Rupert before going on to his glorious defeat at Oxford.

There were further refurbishments made to Castle House in the 1700s, and in the 1830s; the north wing was completely demolished. In 1881 electricity was installed and in 1908 a priest's hole was discovered containing a male skeleton. The skeleton is assumed to be that of a Jesuit priest who became trapped in his hideout and is candidate number three for the Castle House ghost.

In the 1960s the house was owned by John Bristow Bull, a descendant of the Prince of Wales. Because of its convenient position to Silverstone motor-racing circuit, Castle House often played host to famous drivers, John Surtees and Stirling Moss being two of the better known amongst them. It was during their visits in the 1960s that the ghost was at its most active.

CALVERTON

Gib Lane at Calverton is reputedly haunted by a murder victim. In the seventeenth century the wealthy Lady Grace Bennett was famous for her parsimonious habits: Lady Grace was as mean as she was affluent.

Adam Barnes of Stoney Stratford was Lady Bennett's butcher. He became convinced that there must be a cache of money about her house. He burgled the premises but was caught in the act and murdered the miserly lady rather than face being apprehended.

Barnes was caught, convicted and hanged, the gallows being erected in Gib Lane. He was then hung in irons on the same spot until his body and the gibbet totally rotted away. The event is commemorated by a carving on a stone barn wall built on the site at Manor House Farm. The carving shows two gibbets and a date of 1693. It is said that the ghost of Lady Bennett roams the Gib Lane on dark nights.

CHETWODE

The family of Chetwode, owners of the local manor, were entitled to take a toll of local cattle passing along the drift roads at Chetwode and half a dozen neighbouring villages. The family had earned this right for having rid the area of a terrible beast, the wild boar of Chetwode Woods.

History states that as late as the 1850s Sir J.N.L. Chetwode still had in his possession, and regularly exhibited, the jaw of this great animal. It is also said that at a place still known as Boars Head Field the skeleton of an immense animal was unearthed.

DRAYTON PARSLOW

There are a couple of strange little brasses on the floor of Drayton Parslow church, near the chancel; one shows three boys and the other shows no less than eleven young girls. All fourteen children are dressed in Tudor attire. The unfortunate brood were orphaned by the tragic death of their parents, Benet and Agnes Blakenolle. The sad tale of the couple's demise is told in an inscription set in the stone.

Tradition has it that a mighty boar was slain in Chetwode Woods.

The village church at Drayton Parslow has a brass which depicts Benet and Agnes Blakenolle accompanied by their fourteen children.

FENNY STRATFORD

St Martin is the patron saint of Fenny Stratford and it is on his day (11 November) that the six Fenny Poppers, strange little cannons about 7in high and weighing about 20lbs, are fired. This tradition dates back to 1730.

The poppers are loaded with gunpowder and fired at midday, 2 p.m. and 4 p.m. by the application of a red-hot rod. These unique little cannons were presented by Dr Browne Willis to commemorate his grandfather, Dr Thomas Willis, who had lived in St Martin's Lane in the parish of St Martin-in-the-Fields, in London, and died on St Martin's Day in 1675. By an odd coincidence Browne Willis's father, another Thomas, also died on St Martin's Day, in 1699.

GAYHURST

Gayhurst House is situated beside the Ouse. Although briefly owned by Sir Francis Drake, it is better known as the clandestine meeting place of Sir Everard Digby, Robert Catesby and Thomas Winter, the leaders of the conspiracy of the gunpowder plot.

The rather eccentric Victorian architect, William Barnes, constructed a circular lavatory at Gayhurst for the male workers of Lord Carrington. It was later bought as a private house and renamed the Dog House. One wonders if the owners were aware of its history.

There is said to be a tunnel running under a main road at Gayhurst. It runs from one abandoned garden to another and had/has a rather grand pointed entrance adorned with the Carrington crest.

HANSLOPE

Hanslope church spire is 186ft high and can be seen from a least three counties. Grotesque faces and ugly gargoyles gaze unnervingly down from the mighty walls. There are also some interesting inhabitants of the graveyard.

One is an old lady who died in Hanslope at the age of 101 and left 174 relatives to mourn her. Another is the prize-fighter Alexander McKay, a native of Glasgow, who died in 1830 at the age of twenty-six. Mckay had taken up a challenge issued by Simon Byrne or Burn in Salcey Forest. He was knocked unconscious by Bryne and was carried into the Watts Arms where he later died.

Prize-fighting being illegal, Bryne fled the area. However, he was picked up three days later at Liverpool whilst trying to board a boat to Ireland. He was brought

Gayhurst, home of many famous characters, including Sir Francis Drake.

Gayhurst was home to some of Guy Fawkes' fellow plotters.

back to Buckingham and tried for murder. Acquitted and freed, Byrne seems not to have changed his way of life; he died, after losing to another combatant some years later. Although the church authorities strongly objected, a stone was erected on Alexander McKay's grave. It was a clandestine operation carried out under cover of darkness. The stone bears the following epitaph:

> Strong and athletic was my frame,
> Far from my native home I came,
> And bravely fought with Simon Byrne,
> Alas but never to return,
> Stranger take warning from my fate,
> Lest you should rue your case too late,
> If you have ever fought before,
> Determine now to fight no more.

It does not always pay to upset your staff. On 21 July Edward Hanslope Watts was shot and killed by his gamekeeper, William Farrow, as he accompanied his wife home from church. Shortly afterwards, Farrow turned the gun on himself, following his master into eternity. The Watts family had the road to Hanslope Park diverted so that the spot of the murder and suicide could not be seen, thereby it could not be a constant reminder of the disaster. I have read that the actual spot has remained fenced off till this day. I'm obliged to the local Women's Institute for much of the above information.

HARDMEAD

There is a wall monument here illustrating a schooner in full sail. The ship is the *Nancy Dawson*. A local man, Robert Shedden, had the schooner fitted out at his own cost for the specific reason of searching for Sir John Franklin, who was lost with all his men in the Arctic. Shedden was on the other side of the world, in the Far East, when he heard the news. He straightaway passed through the Tropics and forced the tiny *Nancy Dawson* as far north as ships could go. As many as fifteen attempts were made to reach Franklin and his unhappy crew. They had, however, starved to death. The bodies were eventually found after a six-year search. A very disappointed and discouraged Shedden sailed back to his beloved Pacific where he died in 1849 – ironically, just a year before Franklin and crew were discovered.

HAVERSHAM

Set in the chancel floor of St Mary's Church at Haversham is the gruesome image of John Maunsell. The plate shows the skeletal likeness of the local landowner; such images became popular in the late fifteenth century, but few can be found today.

LATHBURY

The Andrews family dwelt in Lathbury House for generations. In 1680 the daughter of the house was the lovely Margaret. At fourteen, young Margaret was ripe for marriage and her suitable suitor was the eighteen-year-old dashing Duke of Somerset. However, as he came to woo his intended, messengers from Lathbury House rode out to inform him that Margaret was very ill; in fact she was thought to be dying. This was indeed the case. Young Margaret lay on her deathbed dividing her not inconsiderable fortune between the poor and the church.

It would seem that the Duke of Somerset finally got over his remorse as he went on to wed Elizabeth Percy who held six baronies in her own right and went on to become the most married woman in England. Elizabeth first became wife and then widow at the age of twelve. She proceeded to marry Thomas Thynne of Longleat and became Duchess of Kent at the ripe old age of fifteen.

LECKHAMPSTEAD

This small village was once divided into two: Leckhampstead Parva and Leckhampstead Magna – the Tween Towns. The manor here is reputed to be haunted. The ghost's gender is unknown, but many of the villagers claim to have seen the spectre strolling by the river. There is also a ghostly report at Weatherhead Farm; this one is reported to carry a spinning wheel.

In 1837 Leckhampstead House was constructed for the Revd Heneage Drummond as a rectory. Drummond was rector to the village from 1835 to 1883. During that incumbency, the Revd Drummond decided that a public house in close proximity to both the church and the rectory was not in keeping with his god-fearing flock. After trying in many ways to close the inn without success he purchased the building and shut it down. Unless they have built one very recently, this charming village is still devoid of a pub.

LILLINGSTONE LOVELL

Lillingstone Lovell remains unspoilt today. It was known as Lillingstone at the time of the Doomsday Book. But in the 1430s it became the property of the Lovell family and their name was added and still remains today.

The spectral lady on a white horse appeared here in 1930s to two old ladies living at Briary, who apparently managed to photograph it. The ghostly lady seems to have put in the occasional appearance over the decades. In fact, as long ago as the 1830s an attempt at exorcism was made. The 1930s appearance, apparently the first for 100 years, became quite a feature with the media. People arrived from Northampton, Oxford, Aylesbury and various other large towns. Unfortunately the photograph of the rider and horse was found to be a fake, which seems to have exorcised the phenomenon for the foreseeable future.

LITTLE HORWOOD

An area in Little Horwood is known today as Shucklow Warren and comes from the Saxon *Scuccan Hlgew*, meaning barrow of the goblins. Within living memory local people still thought it the abode of a gruesome goblin.

Shucklow Warren is supposedly home to a vicious goblin. *(Brenda Allaway)*

MAIDS MORETON

Maids Moreton was once justifiably famous for its Mummers. Dressed in colourful and comical attire they would walk around the village on Boxing Day. Bearing on high various utensils, such as pans and clubs, the marchers would declare:

> Here come I, old Belzebub
> In my hand I carry a club
> Over my shoulder a dripping pan
> Don't you think I'm a jolly old man?

There was once a character in Maids Moreton named Dick Jones who bathed in the glowing nickname of Captain Starlight. Having returned from the First World War, he found he had to leave his cottage in Bachelors Row when his mother died. Obviously having undergone training in the trenches whilst abroad, Dick put this knowledge to good use when he dug a large pit near Chalkmore Farm. He then made a wooden roof, covered it with straw and cut steps down to his subterranean abode where he slept peaceably on sacks of straw. Dick never moved elsewhere and died in his cosy underground domicile.

As to the nickname, Captain Starlight, it is thought to come from Dick's extensive knowledge of the planets and stars. Dick was often seen at night staring at the heavens whilst smoking his pipe.

In one of the most beautiful and peaceful settings overlooking the River Ouse is, or was, a grim reminder of scenes once enacted here. Here stands Hangman's Oak, which contains an iron ring used for the execution of sheep stealers.

MIDDLE CLAYDON

Claydon House was once one of the most magnificent manors of England. Sir Edmund Verney bought the house in 1620; at the time, Sir Edmund mixed in Royal circles. He was appointed and justly earned the title Knight Marshal of the Palace and was also the MP for Wycombe.

Sir Edmund's main entertainment was the betterment of Claydon House. He enthused his carpenter, Luke Lightfoot, to declare he would make the interior 'such a work as world never saw'.

When Civil War broke out, Sir Edmund was in an enigma: he strongly believed in the cause of the Parliamentarians, but was staunchly loyal to Charles. 'I have eaten his bread,' he declared. Verney knew that his loyalty had overcome common sense; he also predicted his own death. He was made Standard Bearer to King

Claydon House at Middle Claydon.

Charles and died at the Battle of Edgehill. His severed hand was found clutching the Royal Standard and was brought back to Claydon for burial. The rest of the popular knight's body was never discovered.

Edmund's son restored Claydon in the better times of 1696. Two years later, his son John, a wealthy merchant, took over the building and was created Viscount Fermahagh. The second Lord Verney, who succeeded in 1752, extended and embellished the house to a princely extent – so much so it beggared him. The contents were seized and Lord Verney fled to France. Some time later, when the house had been tightly shuttered, a stable boy found the earl wandering the corridors. He took him home and concealed him for weeks.

A later Verney, in 1858, took Parthenope Nightingale as his second wife. Parthenope was the elder sister of Florence who was a frequent visitor and later resided at Claydon.

Sir Edmund's ghost is said to haunt Claydon House. He appears on the red stairs and seems to have a bandaged arm. Perhaps he is looking for his severed hand that was interred at the house.

There is also the spectre of a grey lady in the rose room. It is thought that she could be the spirit of Florence Nightingale. Why the famous nurse should be a more favoured candidate than any of the dozens of other female inhabitants is surprising.

In King Charles I time it was rumoured that ghostly armies could be seen re-enacting the Battle of Edgehill on the lawns of Claydon House. The king sent men of sensibility to evaluate the situation. They returned stating that they had witnessed the ghostly scene. Perhaps they were a little prejudicial to please the king's fancy.

NEWPORT PAGNELL

I am indebted to Andrew Green's *Our Haunted Kingdom* for relating the story of the *Buckinghamshire Standard* ghost. Andrew points out, quite rightly, that newspapermen are hard-headed and much inclined to disbelieve anything supernatural. However, the staff of the *Buckinghashire Standard* were working late in St Johns Street, Newport Pagnell, when a definite noise from an empty storeroom above interrupted the folding of newspapers. The workers listened in silence to the definite footsteps and scratching.

We are not informed as to whether anybody had the courage to go and investigate. A previous tenant stated that the footsteps were of no surprise as they had been heard a number of times before. Also, a young printing apprentice, working late, had enquired of his colleagues in the morning, 'Who is the figure in white that watches you through the window?'

OLNEY

Olney was for years the home of the poet William Cowper. There is a strangely shaped monolith, in the market place, which commemorates the town's sons who died in the two world wars. There is also a fifteenth-century church with some really grotesque gargoyles. The pulpit originally came from St Mary's Church, Woolnoth; it was then moved to Northampton prison and finally to Olney. It remains the only pulpit in the country to escape from penal servitude.

Olney is famous for its pancake race. Between 11.30 and 11.45 on Shrove Tuesday morning the pancake bell is rung and the race proceeds as it has, with only a few exceptions, since 1445. The Olney race rules are strict. Competitors must be at least sixteen years old and have lived in Olney or nearby Warrington for at least three months. Aprons and scarves are worn but slacks and jeans are not acceptable. The pancake must be tossed at least three times before reaching the church door. A dropped pancake may be picked up and tossed again. The

Olney, home of eccentric poet William Cowper. John Gilpen, who rode from Edmonton to London, was one of Cowper's comical heroes. *(Brenda Allaway)*

winner receives a kiss from the bell-ringer and both winner and runner-up are presented with prayer books. The race now has an international flavour as Olney is in competition with Liberal, a town in Kansas, USA.

Olney is one of several places in the area that relates the tale of a disputed church site. The foundations of Olney church could originally be found at Lordship Close, near to the site where the building now stands, but the brick work mysteriously disappeared overnight and was discovered at the present site. So often did this happen that the authorities decided to bow to the inevitable and placed the church where it may be seen today.

Although William Cowper is mostly remembered for his comic verse, 'John Gilpen' etc., it must not be forgotten that he also penned some very serious work.

A strange friendship grew between Cowper and John Newton. Newton, strangely an ex-slave trader, became Olney's curate in 1764. Together they produced *Olney Hymns* (the most famous of its hymns being 'Amazing Grace'). Cowper had suffered severe stress and other mental problems since early adulthood. His depression was greatly agitated when his father forbade him from marrying his cousin, Theodora Cowper. In 1763 Cowper had prospects of a job in the House of

Lords. However, the prospect of an examination that he would easily pass caused a mental breakdown and an attempted suicide. Cowper's mental balance improved after years of nursing by Morley Unwin, a clergyman, and his wife Mary. After Morley's death Cowper became engaged to Mary, but after consideration it was decided that due to Cowper's continuing mental ill health the couple should forgo marriage.

In all probability Cowper's state of mind was not improved by his close association with John Newton. Newton was miserable and gloomy, and a dyed-in-the-wool Calvinist. There is little doubt that the ex-slave trader convinced Cowper that he was doomed to eternal damnation and in 1773 he suffered another severe attack of mental aggravation. However, when Newton moved to London Cowper made some improvement.

The demise of Mary Unwin in 1796 resulted in the deepest depression the poet had as yet experienced. It resulted in his last great poem, 'The Castaway'.

PRESTON BISSETT

A cottage near the church was known as Old Hat. The church has figures on the outer wall which include a jester, a monkey and Satan. The chancel area is propped on the backs of two grotesque beings. There is a monument put up to a rector's son who was killed by a tiger in India. These are the four strange claims to fame of this pretty and petite village.

RAVENSTONE

This is the village of the once notorious Lord Chancellor Finch. It is said that he gave much to his village, Ravenstone, but took from his country a great deal more.

After the death of Cromwell, and the dissolving of the Convention Parliament, of which John Milton was a member, the famous poet was held in custody. There was a motion to have him released. Finch, then the Speaker of the House, was far keener to have him executed. However, common sense finally prevailed and Milton, who had been Cromwell's secretary, was set free – a process that many said was aided by the greasing of palms.

Under Finch, England was almost an autocracy. He reached his main ambition at the age of fifty-four when he became Lord Chancellor. So proud and obsessive was Finch of his position, that it is said he slept with the Great Seal under his pillow. It can't have been conducive with a good night's sleep.

SHENLEY CHURCH END

Here it is reputed that a thorn tree blooms on Christmas Eve at midnight. It happened in 1963 and a local newspaper reported of sceptical visitors who became quite surprised when flowers did appear. However, it must be said that the blooms were sparse.

STEEPLE CLAYDON

The Buckinghamshire village of Steeple Claydon has a chirpy little ode about its pubs.

> The Black Horse kicked the Crown
> And drank the Fountain dry
> The Sportsman shot the Prince of Wales
> And made the Phoenix fly.

Unfortunately, the Black Horse shut many years ago. I haven't been in Steeple Claydon for some time, but I shall be surprised if others haven't followed suit.

STEWKLEY / SOULBURY

Boys in Stewkley used to go sparrow netting at dusk. The birds were trapped by putting nets on one side of a bush and bashing the other side with sticks. Sparrow pie was once on the housewives' menu in most villages.

I am indebted to *The Buckinghamshire Village Book* for the information that a house in Ivy Lane was the country abode of Mrs Emily Pankhurst. She retreated here with her daughter Sylvia and probably met many of her colleagues from the Votes for Woman endeavours. Obviously few people knew of her abode, for when she went missing the whole of the country was looking for her.

There is reputed to be a ghost at Stewkley, but information is hard to glean. It is said to be the shade of Revd William Wadley. Old Wadley is described as having a long grey beard and rides his white mare up to the old manor house. On a recent visit to Stewkley, I was unable to find anybody who had actually witnessed the reverend.

In the 1880s a black dog of friendly disposition used to follow a farming family's cart each week on its trip to market. The lane they took between Stewkley and Soulbury was quite well used, but the faithful hound kept pace

"I think you must have scared him off."

Stewkley and Soulbury. In 1865 a spooky black dog regularly followed a farmer's cart here. (*Brenda Allaway*)

with the cart, albeit about 15 yards behind. The family got so used to the occurrence they used to look out for it. One day it was a little closer than usual; the young farmer's daughter jumped down and attempted to pat it upon its head. Working on the basis that you can look but you better not touch, the dog disappeared, never to be seen again.

Robert Hobas was the spiritual leader of Soulbury and Abbot of Woburn. At first he acknowledged Henry VIII as head of the church. However, after seeing Thomas Moore beheaded he changed his mind and gave his allegiance to the Pope. Not a wise move; he paid the penalty in 1538 when he was hanged from an oak adjacent to his own abbey gates.

Soulbury has no ghosts; however, a stone situated on Chapel Hill is reputed to roll down the hill each night when the clock strikes twelve.

STOKE HAMMOND

The old Rectory at Stoke Hammond is reputedly haunted, but by whom or what is unknown. It certainly affected the local parson, and could have been the cause of him making acquaintances with the whisky bottle. The nameless vicar could often be observed making his way from the Dolphin Inn carrying a bag containing several bottles. The parson began to see and hear strange things that were definitely not revelations from the one above. It was where the railway ran closest to the church during his unsteady return home that the parson received some of his most inscrutable messages. He believed that he received coded revelations from the train drivers' whistles as they passed him by.

The landlord of the Dolphin at Stoke Hammond committed suicide when he was suspected of stealing fowls.

Possibly the ale at the Dolphin Inn made people act a little more strangely than ale purchased elsewhere. Early in the last century, when most people kept their own fowl, hens and ducks were disappearing at a steady rate. The landlord of the Dolphin encouraged the villagers to suspect several local boys. One night the owner of Stoke Lodge chased somebody in the act of stealing his poultry, in the dark he threw a spanner and heard it strike home. Several days later the landlord of the Dolphin was discovered hanging from a beam in his stable. Legend dictates that he had a nasty gash on his head.

The Buckinghamshire Village Book relates how Stoke Hammond once had a blind church bell-ringer. By using his initiative he was able to do the work of three people. He pulled one bell rope with each hand and rang a third bell with his foot, a loop having been fixed to the bottom of the rope.

STONY STRATFORD

A lovely little market town is Stony Stratford, sitting on Watling Street where it crosses the Ouse into Northants. Stony Stratford is fighting tooth and nail to withstand the ever capacious and encompassing arms of Milton Keynes. The town was the victim of two fires in the eighteenth century. On the corner of a house, equidistant between the outer limits of the fires, a sundial has been placed. The inscription reads, 'time and fire destroy all things'. I find this slightly ironic as the sundial is opposite an elm tree where Wesley preached of eternal life.

As this was a staging route, there is no shortage of old inns. Here the Cock stands near the Bull. Both hostelries were well frequented in the eighteenth and nineteenth centuries. Also, the lodgers were inclined to tell tall stories of their trips on the road. These tales, greatly exaggerated, gave rise to the expression 'a cock and bull story'.

Stony Stratford, Wesley's tree in the Market Place.

STOWE

Stowe has the most enchanting and numerous follies in the world. There are 221 acres of them. Personally I find it too ambitious to attempt to see them all in one day.

Gibbs' Triangular Temple is arguably the most striking. It is, however, by no stretch of the imagination, attractive. It is an ugly, hideous, rusty brown Gothic construction, which is magnetic in its grotesque appeal.

I wonder why this, of all his many constructions, is the one the genius James Gibbs is said to haunt. There is very little evidence of this and, being hearsay, it is never mentioned in the guidebooks. Of all the other quite beautiful constructions close at hand why should he choose the Temple? At a close distance there are two magnificent arches, three pavilions, three bridges, four obelisk towers and columns. There are seven other temples, three monuments and at least ten other constructions: fountains, caves, grottoes, menageries, etc.

Stowe, the Temple.

Opposite: Inn signs for The Cock and The Bull at Stony Stratford. The two pubs were famous for their exaggerated 'Cock and Bull' stories.

Stowe House.

Swanbourne church. Nearby is a
memorial plate to a murdered man.

SWANBOURNE

Swanbourne's oldest and strangest memorial is the seventeenth-century portrait brass of Thomas Adams. Thomas was a Freeman of London but unfortunately came to grief in 1627, at Swanbourne, where he lived with his wife and four children. Adams was murdered as the memorial states:

> In prime of youth by thieves was slain
> In Tiscombe ground his blood the grass did stain.

All of the family is depicted on the memorial brass. This is how the villagers know the identity of the Green Lady who has haunted the area for over 300 years. She is said to be Elizabeth Adams, who bewails the loss of her beloved husband and searches for his murderers.

TINGEWICK

Tingewick is/was the home of a headless dog. It was photographed by a retired CID inspector in 1916. Copies of the photograph showed two genteel and matronly ladies at afternoon tea whilst a uniformed maid stands holding a milk jug. In the left foreground of the picture is a clear image of a dog. The head seemed to be fading from just above the neck ,or quite possibly it is turned towards the tea table. Other photographs taken shortly before and after show no evidence of the spectral canine. A copy of the image was circulated in the village but the mysterious beast was not recognised as local.

There was something strange about William Stevens, a local tailor in the village of Tingewick. The local girls could not stand him; there was something weird, something you could not put your finger on, something to be left alone. Stevens was not a bad-looking lad of twenty-four. He was also very polite, if a little bit too proud of the tailoring skills he had learnt from two years in London. None of this seemed to compensate for his uncanny stare or from the scandals, true or imagined, that were circulating about him.

Stevens lived next door to seventeen-year-old Annie Leeson, and Annie was less than enchanted when she received a couple of presents from him, on Valentine's Day, in 1864. To stop the imagined relationship before it started, Annie totally ignored him. Smarting and badly wounded mentally by this slight, Stevens began brooding and even began muttering dark threats about Annie to his associates. Unfortunately for the teenager, nobody took him seriously and none of the threats were reported to the authorities. A couple of weeks after his disastrous Valentine's

Day, Stevens noticed his intended victim at the village pump. Straightaway he picked up his razor-dashed across the green and slit Annie's throat with two deep cuts. Annie staggered across the street to the doorway of the shop where she worked and died there shortly afterwards.

In the meantime, Stevens attempted suicide by cutting his own throat. His intention was denied by his own mother and several neighbours who managed to stem the bleeding.

William Stevens' recovery took months, so it was July before he was charged and convicted at the County Assizes. He met his maker on Friday 5 August 1864, on the scaffold outside Aylesbury Prison. An estimated crowd of 4,000 people looked on.

Whilst in his cell awaiting execution it is said that Stevens was greatly despondent and deeply regretted his actions. He died in remorse and admitted the justice of his sentence.

WATER STRATFORD

In the seventeenth century, Water Stratford was the unfortunate choice of abode of John Mason. Mason convinced many people that he was a prophet and that he would die, rise again and bring judgement to the world. His predictions spread like wildfire and his followers turned from hundreds to thousands. Credulous people came from all over the country to live in Mason's makeshift sheds and barns to wait for the end of the world, which Mason had predicted would be in about twenty years time.

Mason was badly affected when his wife died, he was consumed with the conviction that judgement day was close and that Christ would reappear here at Water Stratford. People were selling their houses and all their goods to join Mason's encampment that now covered many acres and was officially known as the Holy Ground. Shrieking, screaming, crying out for redemption, dancing, singing and all manner of hysteria made up Mason's services.

Even when Mason died in 1694, his thousands of disciples would not believe it. The religious hysteria seemed to increase rather than abate. Mason's successor had his body exhumed to prove that he was dead – many remained unconvinced. Finally the Government called in the military to disperse the believers.

WILLEN

Willen was the home base of Richard Busby, probably the greatest teacher of the seventeenth century. Busby was headmaster of Westminster School for half a century. He was known as a mighty flogger and, with the possible exceptions of Dr Fell, of the nursery rhyme, and Dr Valpy of Reading, Busby spent the most time handing out corporal punishment.

However, Busby was extremely successful; he educated generals and admirals and sixteen bishops, not to mention famous giants of literature such as John Dryden. John Lock was also one of Busby's illustrious pupils.

According to Dr Johnson, who knew Busby well, his success was due to 'Busby, birch and benevolence'. He called his rod his sieve and stated that whoever did not pass through it was no boy for him. There is also a story that when Charles II visited Westminster School, Busby forewarned the king that he would not be lifting his hat. This was not in disrespect to the king, but he dared not let his boys think that there was anyone greater than he.

Busby built his church at Willen; it was designed by Robert Hooke, an ex-pupil, and right-hand man to Sir Christopher Wren.

WINSLOW

Winslow Hall, a vast and attractive building in the centre of the village, is thought to be the work of Sir Christopher Wren and dates from 1700. Its original function was that of a hunting lodge.

Keach's Meeting House was built in 1625. Benjamin Keach's abode was the headquarters of the Dissenting Baptists. His crime was to introduce congregational singing in his chapel; this incurred the wrath of the London Baptist Association, who condemned it as 'carnal formality'. For fear of discovery, Keach's chapel was hidden behind larger buildings. I was told there is an atmosphere of peace and tranquillity there and that the building has changed little since its Puritan days. The square has a couple of interesting inns, the George is famous for its intricately designed ironwork, but little is known of its history. John Camp, in his book *Oxfordshire and Buckinghamshire Pubs* (published in 1965), informs us that the Bell has been in the same family for over 150 years. We are told that the family took over the inn in 1814. Camp describes it as 'a large and handsome structure dominating the surrounding buildings'. Nothing has changed that aspect, I can assure you. It is also described as Dickensian and I'll go along with that. It is a charming place. I'd heard about a ghost here, but I could glean no information whatsoever.

Winslow, the tiny Keach's Meeting House was a secret assembly point for the Dissenting Baptists.

Winslow, the reputedly haunted Bell Inn, was owned by the same family for 150 years.

WOLVERTON

I should like to thank Tony Barham's, *Witchcraft in the Thames Valley*, for the following story. There is a legend at Wolverton concerning a witch's curse. The story goes that a local farmer fell on hard times and borrowed money from a witch's son. The man's fortune greatly improved but he refused to repay the borrowed money. He swore a solemn oath that he owed nobody. However, at that precise moment, not one but two of his wagons carrying barley was swallowed up by the earth. Two ponds remain where they disappeared.

WOUGHTON ON THE GREEN

Lying in the churchyard here is an ancient coffin lid and peering out from the church are rampant creatures of comic, and also grim, fancy. One at the north doorway is of particular significance.

There are stories here about the ghost of Dick Turpin. (Dick reputedly haunts over 200 sites, most of them in the vicinities he did not visit in life.) History, however, seems to confirm that the robber did use the village as a hideout. But the story of him forcing the blacksmith at the Swan at Wharton to reverse his horse's shoes to confuse his pursuers is by no means likely. I am no horseman but friends who are tell me it just wouldn't work. Not only that, but there were literally thousands of horses on the roads in those days – to pick out an individual animal would be impossible. Turpin's ghost is, unsurprisingly, thought to be seen here attired in cloak and tricorn hat.

There is a less celebrated ghost, or ghosts, in the area of the old Swan: 'Old Curly and his dog'. The spectre is only scary because of his sudden and quiet appearance. Sometimes alone, but usually with his canine friend, Curly appears from some shrubbery that has come to be known as Curly's Bush.

Other titles published by The History Press

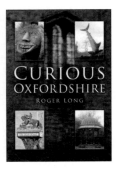

Curious Oxfordshire
ROGER LONG

Curious Oxfordshire is a guide to over 100 unusual and extraordinary sights, incidents and legends from all parts of the country. Featured are unsolved murders, witchcraft, hangings, poltergeists and 'cunning men'. Illustrated with a range of photographs and original drawings, Roger Long's entertaining stories will inspire Oxfordshire residents and visitors alike.

978 0 7509 4957 6

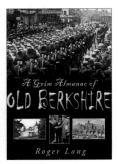

A Grim Almanac of Old Berkshire
ROGER LONG

A Grim Almanac of Old Berkshire includes tales of murder, smuggling, strange deaths, bodysnatching, bizarre disasters and more. Roger Long has investigated archives for evidence of the darker side of Berkshire life and brings his findings together in this day-by-day guide.

978 0 7509 3511 1

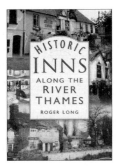

Historic Inns Along the River Thames
ROGER LONG

Historic Inns Along the River Thames features over sixty inns, with potted histories, illustrations and directions on how to find them. It begins in the capital and wends its way along the course of the river, working its way back to the source. It is useful to those with an interest in local and social history.

978 0 7509 4364 2

Literary Buckinghamshire
PAUL WREYFORD

Poet John Betjemen was not the only scribe 'beckoned out to lanes in beechy Bucks'. Many of the country's most famous writers shared his fondness for the county and sought solace within its boundaries. John Milton came here to escape the plague in London; Enid Blyton fled the capital's increasing development, while D.H. Lawrence and his German wife took refuge on the outbreak of the First World War. *Literary Buckinghamshire* offers stories of well-known lives and lost and hidden aspects of the county's history.

978 0 7509 4959 0

Visit our website and discover thousands of other History Press books.

www.thehistorypress.co.uk

The
History
Press